Quadrille

new wave asian

*a guide to the southeast asian
food revolution*

Sri Owen

photographs by Georgia Glynn Smith

For three great cooks,
who have shown me
that true innovators
respect good traditions:
Cheong Liew – Tetsuya Wakuda – Alice Waters

Art Director: Mary Evans
Editor & Project Manager: Lewis Esson
Design: Jim Smith
Photography: Georgia Glynn Smith, except for the photographs on
pages 6 and 7, which are by the author, and the pak choy and choy sum
photographs on page 24 and the photographs on pages 74, 75, 90 and 91,
which are by Tham Nhu Tran
Home Economist and Editorial Consultant: Jane Suthering, assisted by Thom Hughes
Styling: Penny Markham
Production: Vincent Smith and Nancy Roberts

First published in 2002 by
Quadrille Publishing Limited
Alhambra House
27-31 Charing Cross Road
London WC2H OLS

Cataloguing in Publication Data: a catalogue record
for this book is available from the British Library.

ISBN 1 903845 78 5

Printed and bound by KHL Printing, Singapore

contents

introduction

My purpose in this book is to bring the best of Southeast Asian food into modern kitchens anywhere in the world, with a plentiful selection of recipes for dishes that I believe bring out the best of such food as it is cooked today, both within the region and beyond. My approach is entirely pragmatic; I have no cleaver to grind. I have not set out to make a case for 'authenticity' or for 'fusion food', or any other predefined style of cooking. So why have I called this book *New wave Asian*?

To start with, it is not just about Asia. My journeys have taken me to continental Europe, the USA, Canada, Australia and New Zealand. All these areas of the world are becoming more aware of Asian food and are learning to shop for it, cook it and enjoy it. I have been privileged to meet, and eat with, some of the chefs and food writers who are spearheading and recording this movement. They come from many countries, many cultural backgrounds, Asian and non-Asian; some are named in this book, and the book itself is, in part, a tribute to them and their achievement.

Of course, I have had bad experiences too; my research would be incomplete if I had not taken risks. In this culinary revolution, however, the good far outweighs the bad, and I do believe it is a revolution. Ingredients, and the ways people think about, combine and cook them, are changing all the time. This book is a progress report, written very much from my own point of view as a cook obsessed with good food. I am not talking about a trend, a fashion that may disappear as quickly as it came. I am talking about an established change in the way people think about food. It may develop in many ways that we cannot foresee, but it is a permanent change of direction.

However, I do always keep in mind the principles on which so much of Southeast and East Asian cooking is based, particularly the combination and balance of tastes and textures. And before we begin our journey, I shall say a little about how Southeast Asian foodways have come to be as they are.

Taste, texture, balance

Southeast Asia is big, and full of people: it has almost half as much land area as the USA, and almost double the US population. Its landscapes, soils, peoples and cultures are wildly diverse. Yet all my reading and all my travelling – not to mention my cooking and eating – have convinced me that there is an underlying unity in all Southeast Asian cuisines and food habits.

The common language of Southeast Asian food starts with characteristic tastes and flavours. We taste with areas of sensitive skin on our tongues (under the tongue as well as on top) and the soft parts of our throats. Recent research has suggested that as individuals we differ greatly in how many taste buds we are born with, but this does not necessarily mean that one person experiences taste differently from another. In any one mouth, however, buds are specialists, each being

particularly sensitive to one of a small number of basic tastes. These are generally recognized, everywhere in the world, as salt, sweet, sour and bitter. One other, called in Japanese 'umami' and perhaps best translated into English as 'savoury', is also now widely accepted. Chilli-hotness, which is something of an issue in Southeast Asian cooking, is not a taste but a burning sensation that can be felt on any part of the skin.

Much of the sense of taste is actually experienced by our sense of smell. Whereas there are at most half a dozen or so tastes, there are thousands, probably millions, perhaps a theoretically infinite number of aromas. Just as an artist or designer is trained to see and describe colours that to most of us appear almost identical, so we can all train our mouths and noses to be more sensitive and more discriminating. In fact, nearly all of us do this automatically as we grow up, though not many, I suspect, realize their full potential.

All Southeast Asians agree, broadly, that a satisfying dish should offer our palates a well-balanced combination of at least three of the tastes and a harmonious blend of two or three aromas. Trying to cram too many sensations on one plate is not considered clever, least of all by modern cooks who want their ingredients to be fresh and of top quality, and who then insist that they should be cooked for exactly the right length of time and allowed to speak for themselves, unadulterated by superfluous spices. As in so much of contemporary design, simplicity and wit often make the greatest impact. That is not to say that every Southeast Asian recipe can be rustled up in ten minutes from a few ingredients, simply that highly flavoured produce is treated with respect and restraint, and care is taken not to overcook foods whose texture is easily destroyed by too much heat.

The textures in food matter to Asians as much as flavour, and again a well-balanced meal should feature a range and balance of them. Our mouths learn to recognize, not only particular foods but the way they have been cooked, partly by their texture. But simply to say that a dish should include something soft, something chewy and something crisp is to rob the description of all subtlety. To illustrate this, I would ask English readers to imagine their way, forgetting taste and aroma and concentrating solely on texture, through a meal of perfectly cooked roast beef with roast potatoes, Brussels sprouts, thick gravy and Yorkshire pudding, followed by apple pie with cream... Take your time. Now, for us, this immediate contact with what keeps us alive makes the plainest meal a sensuous experience.

There's a further dimension that matters to many folk in Southeast Asia, though it is not so instinctive as those of flavour and texture. They have all sorts of theories about which foods are good or bad for them, and why. Some of these reflect sound observation of the effects of naturally occurring chemicals in foodstuffs. They can be summed up in the classification of foods into those that heat the interior of the body and those that cool it. Most Westerners think of this as a cornerstone of traditional Chinese medicine, allied to the doctrine of yin and yang. This indeed it is, but the idea of 'hot' and 'cold' foods is found in so many parts of the world that one feels it must have arisen spontaneously in several places. Many Southeast Asians are aware of it and accept that healthy eating requires a balance to be struck between heating and cooling, particularly when someone in the family is ill or moody or generally out of sorts.

Tradition and change

One reason for the increasing popularity of Asian food, I believe, is that people in the West are moving away from the three- or four-course 'lunch' or 'dinner' towards the one-course or one-dish meal that Asians have always enjoyed. There is, however, a definite concept of 'a meal' to which, I think, most Asians would subscribe. It usually consists of one main course, followed by fresh fruit or perhaps a Western-style dessert.

The main course is more or less a buffet, which may have just two or three dishes, or twenty for a big party. In any case there is likely to be at least one 'dry' dish, with little or no sauce, and one 'wet' one. There is often a bowl of clear soup, to be eaten with whatever else you put on your plate, almost as Westerners might sip water. There will certainly be a large bowl of plain boiled or steamed white rice; without this, the meal is not a meal at all, just a snack. It is unlikely that these dishes come piping hot from the kitchen, as most Asians dislike food that is too hot to eat comfortably and really don't care much if it has gone cold.

Of course there are exceptions to this pattern. A Chinese banquet, which usually takes place in a restaurant, is served as a succession of individual dishes, something like a tasting menu. And many middle-class professional people in Asian cities have lived in the West and have adopted the standard Western three-course meal, so there is give and take on both sides.

There is nowhere better to watch this than in the lands of the Pacific Rim, above all in the region's two opposite corners – the northwest coast of North America, and in Australia and New Zealand. The great change that has taken place there since 1945 has multiple causes, but a major one has surely been the great Asian Diaspora. Of course, people have been leaving Asia for centuries, but never in conditions that allowed them to have any real impact on the food of the communities in which they settled. There were thousands of Chinese and Indian restaurants, but very few offered authentic Chinese or Indian menus; they adapted or reinvented their dishes to suit Western tastes.

Large, educated, prosperous Asian communities are now firmly established in Australia and New Zealand, Canada (especially British Columbia) and throughout the USA (but particularly from Los Angeles up to Seattle). These newcomers, whether refugees from war or 'economic migrants', have brought with them many of their own traditions and have speedily acquired a mastery of western technology and ways of life. They are growing their own fruits and vegetables wherever the climate allows, and opening their own businesses. This thumbnail sketch of the past half-century is a caricature, certainly, but I think it brings out the salient features that I want to be recognized.

My 'new way'

All the recipes I have ever published, all the meals I have ever cooked, are, I trust, true to the spirit of the tradition in which I was brought up. However, I no longer, in this book or elsewhere, use the old names of traditional or 'classic' dishes in the languages of the countries in which they originated. If you are familiar with Southeast Asian food, you will recognize such dishes in this book, and you may indeed have come across the traditional recipes in my earlier books. Their present forms have been developed by good cooks, professional and domestic, in various parts of the world, and to some extent by myself, since my own cooking, inevitably, is what I'm most familiar with. I have experimented with these dishes, developed them, borrowed from them and combined them, again and again. I have talked and cooked with caring chefs and eaten in their restaurants in Asia, Australia and America, and I have learned greatly from them.

I have sometimes been attacked for ignoring street food, the taste of the people. As a student in Yogyakarta, I practically lived on street food, and there is quite a lot of it in my *Indonesian Food and Cookery* and in *Indonesian Regional*, but I have found that nowadays one has to be choosy. The working conditions on a street food stall or even in a food court are not conducive to good cooking beyond a very simple repertoire of basic dishes. I agree with street food enthusiasts and with five-star chefs that good food starts with first-quality fresh ingredients, and that these should be allowed to 'speak for themselves'. But Asian cooking demands the right choice and subtle mingling of strong flavours. The long lists of ingredients that you find in Asian cookbooks are not made up at random; these herbs and spices are needed to enhance and balance each other.

So my purpose in this book is to explain how these spices and herbs and other ingredients can be made to produce the best results with the least trouble. I try to cook with common sense, not to be authentic just for the sake of it. My curry pastes, for example, are authentic mixes, but I don't hesitate to use a food processor to make my pastes in bulk, and then to store them in ice-cube trays in my freezer. If you do this, you can have instant curry paste whenever you need it. It will taste better than curry paste bought in tubs from the supermarket, it will be more convenient to use as well as cheaper, and you will know exactly when it was made and what went into it.

Presentation is important, too. Good food should appeal to the eye as well as to the nose and palate. The photographs in this book present the dishes in a modern style, 'Westernized' if you like, but without compromising the tastes and textures of the food itself, which is still truly Asian. The photographs are of course only 'serving suggestions'; you are free to present the meal in whatever fashion you like, within whatever limits your circumstances impose. The important thing is that you should feel comfortable with what you are doing.

I end with a few words from two chefs who are right at the top of my pantheon of food gods. Cheong Liew, a Malaysian Chinese by birth, has for many years presided over the kitchen of the Grange Restaurant in the Hilton International, Adelaide. He told me: 'In fact, most of my dishes are original. What I've been saying to a lot of my chefs is, OK, you go to college and learn one side of classical cuisine – that is just not enough. You have to improve, either you get into the Indonesian and Malaysian style of cooking, or the Asian style, Mediterranean, Japanese – they have to know more about all those other cuisines before they can really mix it. And at the same time you've also got to have your heart and soul in all those particular cuisines, because you cannot cook or bring any of those cuisines together unless you understand those cultures very well. I think it's fair to say that - especially in Asia, and a lot of the Mediterranean – we come from a culture where everybody looks after each other, we share, and that is the difference: we should understand other cultures really very easily, and understand their manners – that really helps a lot in capturing the essence of difference.'

And the last word goes to Alice Waters, founder-proprietor of the near-legendary Chez Panisse, across the Bay from San Francisco, who exactly sums up the case for innovation: 'I think that those choices you make about food are choices that you make about the quality of your life, choices that you make about the future. It's a real commitment, but it's a delicious kind of revolution that we're creating in making these good choices.'

Good choices, I hope, are what this book is about.

Sri Owen, London, June 2002

soups and one-bowl meals

People in tropical Asia usually don't drink water with their meals. They say it merely fills you up and makes you feel bloated. On the other hand, warm soup (soups are rarely served cold or chilled) makes you feel comfortable inside and helps digestion, so even at a big meal with many dishes there is always soup, usually a clear broth, on the table. The same broth, with rice or noodles added, will make a simple one-bowl meal, nourishing and comforting. Of course, anyone who is ill is given clear soup with rice in it and soon gets better. There is a gastronomic side to all this, however, and one bowl can offer a basinful of flavour, as you'll see.

creamy chayote and mango soup

Chayote, or choco (Sechium edule, *page 14*), is about the size and shape of a pear, with light, waxy-looking green skin. Its name is Aztec, and it became popular in many tropical areas after Europeans transported plants from Mexico; it grows particularly well at fairly high altitudes, where it gets plenty of rain but not excessive heat. A chayote, like a cucumber, is about 90% water; however, it is eaten cooked, usually as part of, or to accompany, a meat dish. Here I combine it with mango and cream or coconut milk to make a velvety and delicious soup that is very warming when served piping hot in winter, but refreshingly cool chilled on a summer's day. If you can't find chayote, use squash.

for 4-6

2 tbsp groundnut oil
2 shallots, chopped
2 tsp chopped ginger
2 chayote, peeled thinly and then cubed
2 tbsp chopped flat-leaf parsley
2 ripe medium-size mangoes, peeled and the flesh cubed
600 ml / 1 pt coconut milk or 300 ml / ½ pt double cream mixed with 300 ml / ½ pt cows' milk
salt and pepper
a little chilli oil, to garnish (optional)

Heat the oil in a heavy saucepan and stir-fry the shallots, ginger and chayote for 2–3 minutes. Add the parsley and 600 ml / 1 pint water. Bring to the boil and cook on a high heat for 25–30 minutes.

Add the mango and continue cooking for 3 minutes. Add the coconut milk or cream mixture and simmer for 15 minutes. Season with salt and pepper. Remove from heat and leave to stand for 10 minutes.

Put the contents of the saucepan in a blender or food processor and blend until smooth.

Transfer the soup to a saucepan to be reheated and served hot, or leave to cool, then chill to be served cold. If you like, garnish with a little chilli oil.

creamy lentil soup

I developed this soup from a 'comfort food' which in Southeast Asia is usually spiced and would hardly ever be eaten as soup – not the way 'soup' is defined in this book, anyway. In countries nearer India, like Burma and Thailand, such dhal-like lentil stews are very popular.

for 4-6

2 tbsp sesame or olive oil
1 large red chilli, deseeded and finely chopped (optional)
1 tsp finely chopped ginger
3 garlic cloves, finely chopped
1 tsp finely chopped inner part of lemon grass stalk
225 g / 8 oz red lentils, picked and rinsed
115 ml / 4 fl oz thick coconut milk, yoghurt or single cream
salt and pepper
juice of 1 lime (optional)

In a heavy-based saucepan, heat the oil and fry the chilli (if using), ginger, garlic and lemon grass, stirring them continuously, for 2 minutes. Add the lentils and continue stirring these for a minute or two longer. Add 1.1 litres / 2 pints water and cook the lentils on a medium heat, stirring often, for 10–15 minutes.

Add the coconut milk, yoghurt or cream and continue to simmer for 5–8 minutes. Add salt and pepper to taste, take the pan off the heat and leave to cool a little.

Put in a food processor or blender and blend for a few seconds until smooth. Transfer the soup to a saucepan and adjust the seasoning if necessary. This is the time to put in the lime juice, if using it.

Reheat the soup just before serving.

sweetcorn, pumpkin, cassava and rice soup with spinach

This is real 'comfort food', perfect for a family meal. For anyone in the northern hemisphere, it makes a warming winter's day lunch or supper. I first encountered it among the hills of North Sulawesi, one of the Indonesian islands only a few miles from the Equator, and for people there it provides a healthy and hearty breakfast. Needless to say, the best result is achieved when all the ingredients are as fresh as they can be.

Cassava *(Manihot esculenta) grows well in poor soils and positively likes a long dry season, which makes it very suitable for the eastern Indonesian islands. The root tubers taste good, are rich in starch, and contain some protein and vitamin C. These tubers range from small, white-fleshed, sweet-tasting and almost non-toxic, to large (about 60 cm / 2 feet long), yellowish, somewhat bitter and poisonous. Most of the poison (prussic acid) is in the outer layers of the tubers and is removed by peeling. When the tubers are boiled, the enzyme is destroyed and no more prussic acid can be released. Many varieties of sweet cassava can be simply peeled, cut up and eaten raw in salads.*

for 6–8

225 g / 8 oz peeled and cubed cassava
60 g / 2 oz long-grain rice, soaked in cold water for 30 minutes, then drained
225 g / 8 oz peeled and cubed pumpkin or butternut squash
4 corn cobs, kernels removed
225 g / 8 oz young spinach
225 g / 8 oz water spinach, trimmed
1 tsp chopped soft inner parts of a lemon grass stalk
20–30 sweet basil leaves
salt and pepper

Soak the cassava in lightly salted water, then drain. Soak the rice in cold water for 30 minutes, then drain.

Put 1.1 litres / 2 pints cold water in a large saucepan and bring to the boil. Add the cassava and rice, and cook for 8 minutes, stirring often. Add the pumpkin or butternut squash and the sweetcorn. Continue to simmer for about 25 minutes. The mixture is then ready to become the basis of the soup; it can be prepared and cooked to this point a day or two in advance, then refrigerated until needed.

When ready to serve, heat the soup in a saucepan until it is boiling, reduce the heat and stir well. Now add the two kinds of spinach, the lemon grass and the basil leaves, and cook for 2 more minutes. Add salt and pepper to taste, if required. Simmer for another 1 minute and serve piping hot.

①

②

③

staple asian vegetables

Prominent among everyday vegetables in Asia are a handful of tubers. These have a longer history as staples than rice, as they are easy to propagate and grow, can be harvested year-round, and are generally easy to store. On the other hand, most are more or less toxic if eaten raw, and inferior to rice in taste, texture and appearance. Each, however, has its party tricks, a limited repertoire of really tasty dishes or snacks.

Taro (*Colocasia esculentum* or *esculenta*, or *C. antiquorum esculenta*) is also known as coco, cocoyam, eddoe and dasheen. Centuries of breeding have produced many different varieties, hence the many names, but its Pacific Island name, Taro, is the most widespread and perhaps the easiest to remember. It is still the staple food of millions of people, and is popular even where the staple is rice. Its great heart-shaped leaves are a familiar sight over much of tropical Southeast Asia, but it is mainly the big brownish-black tubers that are eaten, sometimes with young leaves and young stems as well. The flesh can be white, yellowish, purple or magenta, and these are colour-fast, not changed by cooking. It is as starchy as a potato and can be cooked in any of the ways that a potato can; taro crisps are becoming a popular snack in the West. Boiled or steamed, taro flesh has a slightly soapy mouth-feel that some Westerners find takes a bit of getting used to.

Sweet potato (*Ipomoea batatas*) is discussed on page 54.

Yam bean or jicama (*Pachyrhizus erosus*) This climbing plant was taken by the Spanish from the Americas to Luzon, thence to Ambon in eastern Indonesia; it is now common in many tropical areas, especially those that are not too wet. It was an immediate success, growing quickly, needing little attention, and producing sweet, starchy tubers that can be eaten raw or cooked (but do peel them first). The seeds are poisonous and so are the leaves. The mauve flowers resemble those of sweet peas. However, growers who want to produce sweet, tender tubers usually prevent their plants from flowering or producing pods or seeds. The tubers are four-lobed, more or less round, flattish on top and tapering to a point underneath, so that from the side they look vaguely heart-shaped. They are obtainable in Chinatowns in most large Western cities, and also in some supermarkets and in Caribbean food stores.

❶ chayote (see page 12); ❷ yam bean; ❸ taro; ❹ sweet potato (see page 54)

avocado and watercress soup
Until recently avocado hadn't been much used in Asian cooking. When 'East meets West' became fashionable 20-odd years ago, though, and more and more people were introduced to guacamole, avocado started to penetrate into middle-class homes via international hotel restaurants. Don't add cream or yoghurt to the blended soup, as they will make the colour too pale.

for 4-6

2 large ripe (but not too ripe) avocados
1 tbsp lemon or lime juice
175–225 g / 6–8 oz watercress
1.1 litres / 2 pt chicken or vegetable stock (page 174)
1 tbsp light soy sauce
1 large green chilli, deseeded and finely chopped
salt and pepper

Peel the avocados, halve lengthwise and stone, then quarter and cube. Put in a glass bowl and add the lemon or lime juice to prevent discoloration. Trim the watercress, discarding hard stalks and wilted leaves. Chop the leaves coarsely and set aside.

Heat the stock in a medium pan and, when it starts to boil, add the soy sauce, avocado, watercress and chilli. Simmer for 4–5 minutes. Taste and adjust the seasoning with salt and pepper. Serve hot, as soon as possible.

Note: if you want this soup to look 'Oriental', serve it as it comes, straight from the pan; otherwise, blend it until smooth for a creamy soup. It can then be served hot or chilled, garnished with cream or yoghurt.

braised scallops in spiced broth with soba noodles
Serve this as a small soupy starter or as a one-bowl lunch or supper. Normally in Southeast Asia the scallops would just be cooked in the soup, almost certainly becoming what Westerners regard as overcooked and slightly rubbery.

for 4, or for 2 as a light meal

115–225 g / 4–8 oz soba noodles
2 tbsp clarified butter or extra-virgin olive oil
8 fresh shiitake mushrooms, halved and stalks removed
salt and pepper
600–900 ml / 1–1½ pt vegetable or chicken stock (page 174)
2 scallops per person, with their corals
a handful of flat-leaf parsley or coriander leaves, roughly chopped, to garnish
lemon wedges, to serve

for the spice mixture

2 garlic cloves
1 bird's-eye chilli
1 tsp dry-roasted coriander seeds
½ tsp coarse sea salt
1 tsp chopped ginger

Heat a pan of unsalted water. When it is just simmering, add the noodles, bring back to the boil, turn down the heat and simmer for 3–4 minutes. Drain in a colander and run cold water over them until they are cold.

Make the spice mixture by crushing all the ingredients together in a mortar with a pestle until fairly fine.

Heat the butter or oil in a medium pan. When hot, add the spice mixture and stir for 30 seconds, followed by the mushrooms. Stir for another 30 seconds, then pour in the stock. Season to taste with salt and pepper and simmer for 3 more minutes. Up to this point, everything can be done several hours ahead.

Just before you are ready to serve, ladle some of the stock into a small saucepan. Bring it to the boil and add the scallops. Cover the pan for 30 seconds only, then take it off the heat. Leave it covered.

To serve, heat the stock with the mushrooms and heat a kettleful of water. When the kettle is boiling, pour it over the noodles in the colander to reheat them. Shake the colander to drain the noodles thoroughly. Divide the noodles among 2 or 4 soup plates and spoon the scallops with their liquid on top, followed by the garnish. Pour equal amounts of the stock and mushrooms over the noodles, and serve straight away, with lemon wedges.

Penang laksa asam

Penang is a small island off the west coast of Malaysia, known to the locals and neighbours as Pulau (meaning 'island') Pinang. For lovers and fans of so-called 'street food' Penang is a prime location, even today, and local people who are exiled (usually as students to Britain and the USA) write nostalgically about it on their Web pages. In fact there are no longer any little street food stalls, or hawkers crying their wares as they roam the city blocks. As in many other Asian cities, street food has been gathered into carefully organized centres, where the authorities can keep an eye on hygiene, which is reassuring. In these places, most of the customers are local residents, with a few tourists looking on and taking more photographs than they order dishes. In fairness, I must say that at centres like Gurney Drive, on the Penang seafront, which starts up at dusk and stays open late, you can eat well at extraordinarily low prices.

This laksa asam (literally, 'sour rice noodles') is still a top favourite in food courts in Malaysia. Here, I describe a traditional soup, but with some less traditional extras: the rice noodles are included, of course, and with them are fish and garnishes that both look and taste good, though you might not find them on Gurney Drive. For the authentic sourness, tamarind water is essential.

for 4 as a substantial soup, or as a one-bowl meal

115 g / 4 oz rice noodles
4 skinless fillets of Dover sole
or sea bass, each weighing
150–175 g / 5–6 oz
1 tbsp lime juice
1 tbsp light soy sauce
a large pinch of cayenne pepper
1.1 litres / 2 pt chicken or fish stock
(pages 174–5)
about 115 ml / 4 fl oz tamarind water
(page 164 – no substitutes, please)
4 tbsp Laksa Paste (page 169)
2 tbsp finely chopped chives
or flat-leaf parsley
salt

for the garnish
8 slices of mooli (white radish),
each cut into a triangle
8 slices of carrot, each cut into a triangle
4 fresh scallops with the corals
a little olive oil
4 tiger prawns, butterflied
and deveined (page 114)

Soak the rice noodles in boiling water for 3 minutes, then drain in a colander, refresh under cold running water until cold and drain again.

Rub the fish fillets with lime juice, soy sauce and cayenne pepper. Keep them in a cool place for up to one hour before cooking them.

Put the stock, tamarind water and laksa paste in a saucepan. Bring to the boil and simmer for 5–8 minutes. Add the chives or parsley and salt. Taste and adjust the seasoning with more salt and tamarind water if necessary. Add the fish fillets and cook in the broth for 3 minutes, then scoop them out and place on a large plate.

Just before serving, prepare the garnishes: blanch the triangles of mooli and carrot for 1 minute in boiling lightly salted water and refresh in cold water, then set aside. Sauté the scallops in the olive oil for 1–2 minutes only, followed by the prawns, and set aside also.

Reheat the noodles in the colander by pouring boiling water from the kettle over them. Heat the broth until just below the boil and add the fish fillets, scallops, prawns and the rest of the garnishes. Keep the fish etc. in the pan for 1 minute, then turn off the heat.

Divide the reheated noodles equally among 4 large soup plates. Then ladle the broth over the noodles and divide the fish and everything else equally. Eat while good and hot!

Cambodian hot-and-sour seafood soup

Of all the hot-and-sour soups of Southeast Asia, this is probably the least complicated to make. Two chefs at the Grand Hotel d'Angkor showed me how to prepare and cook it. The fish they used was, of course, a freshwater species, for Siem Reap is just a few kilometres from the Tonle Sap, the 'Great Lake' that has supplied the Khmers with fish and watered their rice fields for 2,000 years. In England, I make this soup with carp or grouper, when I can get them. Failing one of those, my choice would be sea bass. Freshwater prawns can be bought frozen (and must of course be thawed completely before cooking). I was very surprised to find the chefs using lime juice as a souring agent instead of the tamarind water more traditional in Cambodia.

for 6–8

1.4 litres / 2½ pt Quick Fish Stock (page 175)

175 ml / 6 fl oz fish sauce (nam pla)

about 175 ml / 6 fl oz lime juice

1–2 tbsp sugar

2–4 bird's-eye chillies, chopped

7 oz / 200 g chopped lemon grass

60 g / 2 oz fresh turmeric, peeled and sliced

100 g / 3½ oz galangal (page 109), peeled and sliced

salt and pepper (optional)

30 g / 1 oz black fungus or 115 g / 4 oz fresh shiitake mushrooms

600 g / 1 lb 4 oz skinless fillets of white fish of your choice, thinly sliced

12–16 shelled fresh tiger prawns, deveined

to garnish

2–3 kaffir lime leaves, shredded

1–2 large red chilli(es), deseeded and thinly sliced

Put the fish stock, fish sauce, lime juice, sugar, chillies, lemon grass, turmeric and galangal into a large saucepan. Bring them to the boil and simmer for 5–8 minutes. Take off the heat, cover and set aside for 10 minutes.

Strain the cooling stock into another saucepan and discard the solids. Taste, and add salt and pepper if necessary. Also add more lime juice to taste, if necessary.

If using the black fungus, soak them in hot water for 5 minutes, then drain and rinse them. Slice into tiny sticks. If using fresh shiitake, just slice them similarly.

To serve, heat the stock until it is just about to boil. Add the black fungus or shiitake mushrooms and bring to the boil. Turn down the heat a little, add the fish and prawns, and simmer for 3–4 minutes. Add the garnishes, and serve the soup straight away, dividing the fish and prawns equally among individual soup bowls.

white crab meat in hot ginger and tamarind broth

Spinach or watercress adds a pleasing bitterness to the complex flavour of this soup. The Chinese heat of ginger with the Indian bite of tamarind is the essence of Asian new wave flavouring.

for 4

850 ml / 1½ pt vegetable stock or
chicken stock (page 174)
4 tbsp tamarind water (page 164)
2 tsp ginger juice (page 109)
1 garlic clove, crushed (optional)
1 tsp coarse sea salt or 1 tbsp light soy
sauce or fish sauce (nam pla)
pepper
225–350 g / 8–12 oz white crab meat
225–350 g / 8–12 oz spinach
or watercress
a handful of flat-leaf parsley
4 spring onions, then cut into thin rounds

Put the stock, tamarind water, ginger juice and garlic into a saucepan, bring to the boil and simmer for 3 minutes. Taste, and adjust the seasoning by adding salt, soy sauce or fish sauce and pepper as necessary.

Add the crab meat and the spinach or watercress. Continue cooking for 1 minute, then add the parsley and spring onions. After 30 seconds, turn off the heat and serve straight away.

soba noodle soup with tempura prawns

Soba is one of those types of noodle that are equally good eaten cold, warm or hot. The idea of serving tempura prawns or vegetables with a soup is quite untraditional, but has been growing in popularity as a means of adding more texture to soups.

for 4

1 tbsp mirin (Japanese rice wine)
1 tbsp sake
1.1 litres / 2 pt Quick Fish Stock
(page 175)
salt and pepper
225 g / 8 oz soba noodles
3 spring onions, thinly sliced, for garnish

for the tempura prawns
16–20 shelled large king prawns, cut in
half lengthwise and deveined (page 114)
about 600 ml / 1 pt groundnut or
sunflower oil, for frying

for the tempura batter
1 egg yolk
175 ml / 6 fl oz ice-cold water
115 g / 4 oz plain flour
salt

Prepare the soup by adding the mirin and sake to the stock. Simmer for 2 minutes, turn off the heat and set aside.

Prepare the noodles: cook them in a pan of gently boiling water for 3–4 minutes, refresh under cold running water and drain well in a colander.

Make the tempura batter: whisk the egg yolk in a bowl until well blended, then add the ice-cold water. Sift the flour and a large pinch of salt into the bowl and stir gently with a fork or a pair of chopsticks. Don't beat the batter – it is supposed to be a bit lumpy; if overmixed it will be heavy.

When ready to serve, reheat the stock and season to taste. Leave to cool to room temperature if serving the noodles cold. Divide the noodles among 4 large bowls and pour over the warm soup. Garnish with the spring onions.

Heat the oil in a wok or small pan (see page 63). One at a time and using chopsticks, plunge the prawns in the batter and carefully lower into the hot oil, in batches of 2–3. Cook each batch for 2–3 minutes and transfer them to a plate lined with kitchen paper. Continue until all the prawns are fried.

Serve these in separate small bowls. If preferred, the prawns can be piled on top of the soup, but then eat straight away as they quickly go soggy.

Simon Yung's 'eight treasures' soup in golden melon

*One of my earlier books had a section on Chinese cooking and in researching it I learned a lot by watching Chef Simon Yung in the Chinese kitchen of the Dorchester Hotel in London. A few years later I met him again, almost by chance, in Singapore, where he is the Head Chef of the renowned Empress Room restaurant in the Raffles Hotel. This is my version of the soup that I enjoyed so much on that occasion. The broth can be either chicken stock or vegetable stock, and the 'eight treasures' you can choose for yourself: they can be all vegetarian, or you can do as I suggest here and put in some lobster tail meat or small scallops. The melons can be honeydew or Charentais, though in Asia they are usually golden watermelons. Choose a size that will make a big enough 'soup bowl' when the melons are cut in half, or small enough for one person when the tops have been sliced off. The delicious **pea shoots**, also called 'mangetout leaves', are the tips of the pea plant. Widely available in Chinatown greengrocers, they are also now to be found in some better supermarkets. They need only to be wilted in the hot soup, and are delicious raw in salads.*

for 4 as a first course, or 2 as a one-bowl light lunch or supper

2 medium-size melons or 4 small ones (see above)
1.4 litres / 2½ pt chicken or vegetable stock (page 174)
1 tbsp melted butter or groundnut oil
salt and pepper
1–2 tbsp light soy sauce
1 tbsp lemon juice (optional)

for the treasures
115 g / 4 oz fresh shiitake mushrooms, sliced
115 g / 4 oz French beans, thinly sliced at an angle
6–8 heads of baby sweetcorn, each cut at an angle into 3
6 spring onions, thinly sliced at an angle
a handful of picked coriander leaves
about half of the flesh of the melons
60 g / 2 oz pea shoots
2 small scallops or 60 g / 2 oz lobster tail meat per person

Wash the melons under cold running water and dry them with kitchen paper or a tea towel. If they are medium-size, cut each in half and scoop out the seeds. If small, cut off the stem end to make an opening big enough for you to take out the seeds and flesh and for the diner to get at the soup. Scoop out the flesh with a melon baller (the half not used in the soup can be served as dessert in a mixed fruit salad). Scrape out the remaining flesh with a spoon and chop it, to be put into the soup with the melon balls. If you are using golden watermelons, pick out the seeds and discard.

Put the stock in a saucepan and bring it to the boil slowly on a medium heat.

Meanwhile, heat a little butter or groundnut oil in another pan, and sauté the mushrooms, beans, baby sweetcorn and spring onions for 2 minutes. Add soy sauce and salt and pepper to taste and stir for another minute.

Transfer the vegetables to the stock and simmer for 5–8 minutes more. Now add the coriander leaves, half the melon balls and the chopped flesh. Continue cooking for 2 more minutes, then add the pea shoots and lemon juice if using. Add more salt if necessary.

If using scallops, slice them across into thin rounds and divide them equally among the melon halves. If using cooked lobster tail meat, divide that similarly. Then pour or ladle the soup into the melon containers, and serve piping hot.

chinese greens

Asian brassicas originated in China and are still thought of as Chinese. There is no general agreement yet on their English names, so these can be a little confusing. There are at least five varieties that we need to be familiar with, and some of these are illustrated here.

Chinese leaves (*Brassica pekinensis*) These may also be labelled Chinese, Peking or celery cabbage. The white stem can be cooked separately from the leaf, sliced fairly thickly then stir-fried with garlic and ginger. Season with soy sauce and pepper or cayenne pepper if you like it hot. The leaves can be added a minute or two before the end of cooking. Stems and leaves are also used in soup, or raw in salads. Whole large leaves can be used to wrap minced meat or fish for steaming.

Little white cabbage (*B. chinensis*) This is the familiar pak choy. It needs very little cooking, but is not good raw. As a variation from stir-frying or braising, I like young pak choy wrapped in ham or bacon and pan-fried for 4–5 minutes. Serve as a side dish or as a starter with your favourite dipping sauce.

Gai lan or Kailan (*B. alboglabra*; also called Chinese broccoli) Full of vitamin C, this grows all year round and is well established in the West. I like it steamed with prawns and served with an oyster sauce dip.

Choy sum (*B. chinensis* var. *parachinensis*) This is recognizable by its dark green leaves, paler stems and bright yellow flowers. Stems and leaves are blanched in boiling water or meat stock, and served with a dipping sauce or Coconut Sambal (page 160). Alternatively, you can stir-fry them with mushrooms and shredded cooked chicken meat, or simply top with crisp bacon rashers.

Gai choy, Chinese mustard greens or mustard cabbage (*B. juncea*) This can be used as a substitute for pak choy. I like to stir-fry it with julienned pork or beef and some fermented black or yellow beans. Like other mustardy brassicas, this has the reputation of stimulating your stomach walls and aiding digestion.

❶ pea shoots (see page 22); ❷ water spinach (see page 28); ❸ little white cabbage or pak choy; ❹ choy sum; ❺ Chinese leaves

chicken soup with glutinous rice dumplings

I have learned so much from Jereme (pronounced Jeremy) Leung of the Four Seasons Hotel in Singapore that I even dare, now, to make savoury sticky-rice dumplings. The tradition in Southeast Asia is that dumplings made of glutinous rice flour are served and eaten as sweets at tea time. In this chicken soup, however, we have glutinous rice dumplings made as Jereme made them for me on a recent visit to Singapore. His soup, I have to say, was different from mine in its textures, being well filled with scallops and large prawns, but he added, as I do, some spinach at the end of cooking, to give another colour and flavour.

for 4-6

15 g / ½ oz butter
115–175 g / 4–6 oz skinless chicken breast meat, cut into small, thin slices
1 tsp finely chopped ginger
1 tsp finely chopped garlic
1.1–1.4 litres / 2–2½ pt good chicken or vegetable stock (page 174)
salt and pepper
275 g / 10 oz young spinach leaves

for the dumplings
275 g / 10 oz glutinous rice flour
70 g / 2½ oz vegetable shortening
100 g / 3½ oz Cheddar cheese, cut into 12 cubes

To make the dumplings: in a bowl, mix the flour, shortening and 300 ml / ½ pint cold water. Knead this mixture until it becomes a soft dough. Divide the dough into 12 portions. Roll each piece of dough into a ball, lay it on a flat surface and flatten it by pressing with the palm of your hand. Put a piece of cheese in the centre of each disc, then roll the dough around the cheese so that you have round dumplings with the cheese hidden inside.

Cook the dumplings in boiling water, in batches of 4–6, for 5–7 minutes each, or until they float to the surface. Keep the cooked dumplings in a bowl of warm water.

To make the soup: heat the butter in a saucepan, stir in the chicken slices, ginger and garlic, and keep on stirring for 2 minutes. Add half of the stock, bring to the boil and simmer for 6–8 minutes until the chicken is cooked through.

Add the remaining stock and season with salt and pepper. Bring back to the boil, then add the spinach. Drain the dumplings and add to the soup. Heat through for 20 seconds, then serve.

new-style mulligatawny soup

This spicy rich, almost earthy soup is my way of cooking what Tamil people call milagu tannir, *'pepper water'. Peppery it may be, but there is nothing watery about it. I have eaten this soup in many places during my travels in the East. I like to cook it and serve it at home as a small first course, but it is ideal as a one-bowl lunch or supper with plain boiled rice. The rice can be served separately, or simply stirred into the soup. Unlike the usual dense flour-thickened soups, my version is much lighter.*

**for 5–6 as a one-bowl meal,
or 8–10 as a first course**

**1 free-range chicken, the breast
part removed, the remainder
cut into 4–6 pieces
85 g / 3 oz dried chickpeas, soaked in
cold water overnight, then drained
(or a small 200 g / 7 oz can of
chickpeas, drained and rinsed)
4 tbsp plain runny yoghurt
salt and pepper**

for the spice mixture
**½–1 tsp cayenne pepper
2 tsp dry-roasted coriander seeds
1 tsp dry-roasted cumin seeds
½–1 tsp ground turmeric
2 cloves
4 shallots, chopped
2 garlic cloves, chopped
2 tsp chopped ginger
1 tsp whole black peppercorns
1 tsp salt
2 tbsp groundnut or corn oil**

to garnish
**2 lemons, peeled, halved lengthwise
and thinly sliced
a handful of basil leaves
1 large red chilli, deseeded and
cut into very thin rounds**

Put the chicken breast and pieces in a large saucepan with 1.75 litres / 3 pints of cold water. Add the drained fresh chickpeas (if using canned, don't add until later). Bring to the boil, turn down the heat slightly and cook for 20 minutes. Take out the breast meat and set aside to get cold, then refrigerate so that it can be cut into neat thin slices. Continue cooking the stock with the rest of the chicken on a low heat for 50–60 minutes (or until the chickpeas are tender).

Strain the stock into another pan. Keep the thigh and drumstick meat, if you wish, to add to the breast meat when serving the soup as a one-bowl meal, or to use in another dish. Discard bones and skin. Collect the chickpeas in a bowl.

Make the spice mixture by putting all the ingredients in a food processor or blender with 2 tablespoons of cold water and blending until smooth. Transfer to a heavy pan and cook gently, stirring often, for 5–8 minutes. Add about 2 cups of the stock and the chickpeas (if using canned, put them in now), and simmer for 4 minutes. Put this mixture into the blender, leave it to cool for a few minutes, then blend it smooth. Pass through a sieve and add it to the remaining stock in the first pan. To this point, everything can be prepared up to 24 hours ahead and refrigerated until needed.

When ready to serve, take out the breast meat from the fridge and slice it thinly, across the grain. Bring the thickened stock in the saucepan to the boil and simmer for 5 minutes. Add the sliced chicken breast and continue to simmer for 2–3 minutes. Now beat the yoghurt with a fork and pour it into the soup. Taste, and adjust the seasoning with salt and pepper. Continue heating the soup for 2 more minutes, stirring all the time.

Serve hot, with the slices of chicken divided equally among the bowls and floated on the soup. Sprinkle the garnishes on top.

Vietnamese hot-and-sour soup of duck and bamboo shoots

Hot and sour make up the favourite combination for all savoury cooking in Southeast Asia. This is certainly so in soups – everyone knows the Thai tom yam. There are hot-and-sour soups in China, in Myanmar (though they don't like it too hot there), in the Philippines and Indonesia. They don't always use the word 'soup', however. What follows, for example, is a one-bowl meal to feed an entire family from a single duck. In the original, the whole duck was chopped up and boiled, bones and all, for several hours. Towards the end of cooking, when the meat was ready to fall off the bones, rice or noodles and a selection of vegetables were added. I have simplified the process to produce a starter for 4 people, or a meal for 2 if you add some rice or noodles to the soup before it comes to table.

__Water spinach__ (Ipomoea reptans or I. aquatica, page 25) is grown throughout the tropics, wherever there is plenty of water or swampy ground (it is sometimes called swamp cabbage, though it is nothing like a cabbage). The young shoots and leaves (sometimes thin and straight, sometimes heart-shaped, depending on variety) can be cooked and served much like spinach, though the two plants are from different botanical families. Water spinach, closely related to the sweet potato, contains traces of iron and is said to be a mild laxative.

for 4 as a first course or 2 as a main meal with rice or noodles

1.1 litres / 2 pt chicken stock (page 174) or cold water
5 cm / 2 in piece of ginger, thinly sliced
1 lemon grass stalk, cut across into 3
1 tsp chilli flakes
salt and pepper
3 tbsp lemon juice or lime juice
1 tsp fish sauce (nam pla)
2 large duck breasts, with skin
2 tbsp groundnut oil
60–115 g / 2–4 oz sliced bamboo shoots
175 g / 6 oz water spinach, trimmed
1 or 2 limes, cut into wedges, to serve
Crisp-fried Ginger (page 170), to garnish

Put the stock or water into a large saucepan with the ginger, lemon grass, chilli flakes and salt and pepper to taste. Bring to the boil and simmer for 20 minutes. Strain into another pan and add the lemon or lime juice and fish sauce. Set aside.

Discard some of the skin and fat from the duck and slice each breast very thinly across the grain. Heat the oil in a wok or frying pan and fry the slices for 3–4 minutes. Remove them to a colander and let the fat drain off.

Heat the stock until it is boiling and add the duck meat. Reduce the heat and continue cooking the meat in the broth, just bubbling gently, for 5 minutes. Add the bamboo shoots and water spinach, and continue cooking for 5–8 minutes longer.

Serve immediately with lime or lemon wedges and garnished with Crisp-fried Ginger.

snacks
and starters

In Southeast Asia, there is no tradition of holding early-evening drinks parties. You may find them among the Westernized urban middle classes. However, we are as familiar as anyone with the snacks and the sort of finger-food I expect to find coming around with the drinks in London, and just, I think, as expert and inventive. This may be partly because of our long tradition of eating between meals and in the street. Foreigners tend to romanticize street food in the same way that, say, French peasant food is romanticized. I am sceptical. These ways of eating have their roots in deprivation; their great traditions are in the cunning use of raw materials, especially offal, that don't appeal much today, certainly not at cocktail parties. I must add, though, that in any Asian town, if you know where to go, you can usually find excellent food being sold by a few street vendors – but you need that local knowledge.

Maluku fish cakes with spiced prawns

Maluku is the Indonesian name for the group of islands known in English as the Moluccas. There these fish cakes are traditionally made with mackerel and cooked until quite rubbery in texture, but here they are lightly cooked and more delicately spiced. My twist is to suggest that you serve them with spiced tiger prawns, the combination making a very appetizing starter.

The best way to cook these fish cakes is in a deep-fryer as, if this is done well and quickly in oil that is good and hot, they actually absorb less fat than they would if pan-fried. If you prefer not to deep-fry, however, you can pan-fry them for 3 minutes on each side and grill the prawns for 2 minutes on each side.

The Fresh Tomato Sambal which, untraditionally, uses uncooked vegetables, acts as a garnish and highlights the sweet, sour and hot tastes of the dish.

for 8 as a starter or 12–16 as canapés

16 large raw tiger prawns, tails on but shells and heads removed, deveined
450 g / 1 lb skinless mackerel fillets
white of 1 egg
1 tsp cornflour dissolved in 1 tbsp water
groundnut or sunflower oil, for frying
Fresh Tomato Sambal (page 162), to serve
flat-leaf parsley, mint or coriander leaves, to garnish (optional)

for the spice mixture
4 tbsp tamarind water (see page 164)
115 g / 4 oz blanched almonds, chopped
3 tsp coriander seeds, roasted (see page 166) then roughly crushed
2 tsp cumin seeds, roasted (see page 166) then roughly crushed
2–4 fresh or dried bird's-eye chillies, chopped
2 garlic cloves, chopped
2 tsp chopped ginger
4 shallots, chopped
1 tsp chopped fresh galangal (page 109)
1 tsp chopped lemon grass (soft inner part only)
1 tsp brown sugar
1 tbsp groundnut or sunflower oil
1 tsp fish sauce (nam pla)
½ tsp salt

Well ahead, make the spice mixture by putting all the ingredients in a blender and processing until smooth. Divide between 2 glass bowls. Put the prawns in one and mix them well with the spice mixture. Cube the mackerel fillets and add them to the other bowl. Leave both to marinate for 4 hours.

Make the fish cakes: put the fish with its marinade into a blender, add the egg white and cornflour mixture, and blend for a few seconds only. Fry a teaspoonful of this mixture and taste it to see if it needs more salt. Divide the mixture into 16 or 24-32 portions. On a piece of baking parchment, roll each portion into a ball and flatten it a little with the palm of your hand.

The best way to fry the fish cakes and prawns is in a deep-fryer. Heat the oil to 160ºC / 325ºF, put 5 or 6 fish cakes into the basket and plunge them into the hot oil. Leave them there for 60–70 seconds only, then take them out and drain on kitchen paper. They will be a rich golden colour. Repeat until all the fish cakes have been fried. The prawns can be cooked in just two batches. Fry each batch in the hot oil for 1 minute only.

To serve as canapés: arrange the prawns and fish cakes on a platter, with the tomato sambal in a bowl as the dipping sauce. To serve as a starter: divide the fish cakes among the plates, top with the prawns and pour the tomato sambal over. Garnish with flat-leaf parsley, mint or coriander leaves, if you wish. Serve warm, with the sambal at room temperature, not chilled.

Filipino palm heart rolls

This is another variation on the so-called 'spring rolls' that are so widespread in Asia and beyond. These are said to be descended from the 'spring cakes' of Tang-dynasty China, which were stuffed with the first fresh vegetables of spring, something to celebrate after the hardships of the northern Chinese winter. It is a little ironic that spring rolls should now be so popular in tropical Asia, where you can get fresh produce at any time of year, but such a brilliant idea for finger food and snacks could not be overlooked.

At one time, pancakes were used as wrappers, but by wrapping the spring roll in pastry and deep-frying it we surround the filling with an extra layer of crispness. It then becomes necessary to ensure that no oil penetrates the wrapper. The best and most practical wrappers to use are, not surprisingly, Chinese spring roll wrappers, which are easily obtainable from the freezer of any Chinese grocer or Oriental supermarket. This version of the spring roll is a Filipino creation; its local name is lumpiang ubud. *Here I will show you how to parcel up the palm heart, or its substitute, in a neat oil-proof purse.*

makes 12–16

12–16 spring roll wrappers, about 12 cm /
5 in square
white of 1 egg, lightly beaten
vegetable oil, for deep-frying
chilli sauce or other dipping sauce of
choice (see pages 158–9), to serve

for the filling
2 tbsp vegetable oil
3 shallots, finely chopped
1–2 large red chillies, deseeded
and finely chopped
2 garlic cloves, chopped
225 g / 8 oz canned palm heart
or bamboo shoots, drained and rinsed,
then cut into tiny julienne strips
(in countries where you can get fresh
palm heart, of course, use this)
115 g / 4 oz French beans or mangetout,
sliced thinly at an angle
115 g / 4 oz ham (the best available),
cut into tiny julienne strips
6 uncooked tiger prawns, shelled,
deveined (page 114) and finely
chopped
1 tbsp light soy sauce
salt and pepper
1 tsp cornflour, dissolved in
1 tbsp cold water

First make the filling: heat the oil in a frying pan or wok, add the shallots, chillies and garlic, and stir-fry for 1 or 2 minutes. Add the palm heart or bamboo shoots and the beans or mangetout, and stir-fry for 2 minutes. Add the ham, prawns, soy sauce and salt and pepper to taste. Continue to simmer this mixture, stirring often, for 3 more minutes. Turn off the heat and stir in the cornflour mixture. Give the whole thing another stir to let the cornflour bind it and leave to cool.

Place a spring roll wrapper on a flat surface and put a tablespoonful of filling in the centre of it. Brush egg white on the wrapper around the filling. Then, lifting one long edge, fold the wrapper up and around the filling, and press together the parts painted with egg white so that they stick and seal the packet. Continue until all the filling and wrappers are used.

Heat the oil in a wok or deep-fryer and fry the parcels in batches of 4 for about 2–3 minutes each batch, until brown and crisp. Serve straight away, with a dipping sauce of your choice.

pan-fried scallops in garlic and chive sauce

You are quite right if you think you won't get this in the food courts of Penang or Malacca, but it is not unusual nowadays to see scallops served in upmarket restaurants, with Thai or Cambodian green papaya or green mango salad. However, I prefer my scallops lightly cooked and eaten without too many other distractions. I would place my fried scallops on a lettuce leaf, or on the shell, with a tiny amount of this sauce.

for 4

8 very fresh scallops with the corals
fine sea salt
3 tbsp groundnut oil
a few drops of sesame oil
1 tsp soft butter
firm lettuce leaves, to serve

for the garlic and chive sauce
2 garlic cloves, crushed
3 tbsp finely chopped chives
2 tbsp hot water
1–2 tbsp lime juice
1 tsp fish sauce (nam pla)
salt and freshly ground white pepper

First make the sauce: put all the ingredients except the salt and pepper in a small pan. Set over medium heat and stir for 2 minutes. Taste and add salt if necessary, then add lots of freshly ground white pepper.

Clean the scallops, pat them dry and sprinkle with a very tiny amount of fine sea salt. If the scallops are large, slice them across their thickness in two discs.

Heat the oils and butter in a frying pan until fairly hot and fry the scallops in the mixture for 1 minute on each side, turning them once.

Serve as suggested above, spooning the warm sauce over the scallops, and eat immediately.

oyster fritters with Thai piquant dressing

Lovers of oysters may think it sacrilege to cook them, but they are almost never eaten raw in Asia. These are no ordinary fritters; they are delicious at any time, and especially so when served as a starter.

for 3-4

115 ml / 4 fl oz groundnut or olive oil,
for frying
12–16 shelled oysters
crisp salad leaves
Thai Piquant Dressing (page 158)
flat-leaf parsley, to garnish

for the coating
4 tbsp plain flour
1 tsp salt
½ tsp cayenne pepper
1 medium carrot, grated
2 tbsp chopped flat-leaf parsley
1 large egg, lightly beaten

First prepare the coating: sift the flour, salt and cayenne pepper into a bowl. In another bowl, mix the carrots and parsley with the beaten egg.

Heat the oil in a non-stick frying pan. One at a time, toss the oysters in the seasoned flour, then dip them in the egg mixture and fry until golden brown (3–4 minutes), turning the fritters several times. Remove with a slotted spoon and drain on kitchen paper. Repeat until all the oysters are fried. Alternatively, you can deep-fry the fritters in a deep-fryer (see page 63); each batch of 4–5 will require 1–2 minutes only.

Serve on a bed of crisp lettuce leaves, dressed with this exquisite, mildly fiery dressing and garnished with some parsley leaves. Alternatively, you can roll each fritter inside a salad leaf, dip it in the sauce and eat it while the oysters are still hot.

Philippines beansprout and prawn fritters

This is a most delicious snack, based on one which in the Philippines is called ukoy *and usually appears at tea time. However, I wanted my version to be served with pre-dinner drinks, so I've made it spicier than the original and replaced minced pork and whole prawns with chopped tofu, minced prawns and grated carrots. These fritters can be deep- or shallow-fried; if you are making a lot of them for a party, however, I recommend deep-frying in a fryer or a wok (see page 63), just for the sake of speed. No dipping sauce is needed.*

makes 40–50 small ukoy to be served as canapés

225 g / 8 oz raw medium prawns, shelled and heads removed
225 g / 8 oz beansprouts, rinsed and patted dry with kitchen paper
3 carrots, grated then squeezed dry
450 g / 1 lb tofu, chopped then squeezed to get rid of excess water
2 tbsp rice powder
2 tbsp cornflour
2 tsp baking powder
½ tsp cayenne pepper
2 tsp ground coriander seeds
2 tbsp chopped spring onions
1 tsp salt
freshly ground black pepper
1–2 eggs, lightly beaten
vegetable oil, for frying (at least 600 ml / 1 pt for deep-frying)

Mix all the ingredients except the oil in a bowl, adding the eggs last. Mix thoroughly by hand. Roll small equal quantities of the mix into small balls. There should be enough for 40–50.

Heat the oil in a deep-fryer or wok (see page 63). Flatten each of the small balls a little between the palms before putting them into the hot oil about 10 at a time and frying each batch for 2–2½ minutes. Lift out and spread on kitchen paper to drain. (If you choose to shallow-fry them in a wok or frying pan, the process will take longer.) They should emerge crisp and golden brown, ready to be served hot, warm or cold.

minced chicken satays with satay sauce

Satay sauce usually means Peanut Sauce or Soy Sauce with Chillies (page 159). Why do I mince the chicken for this satay? Usually I like the taste of a dish with which I am familiar. When I was a little girl, chicken satay with peanut sauce was for me exactly what fish and chips with tomato ketchup became to my two sons when they were in primary school in England. Here, on top of the usual ingredients, I am adding two new flavours to the marinade for the minced chicken – lots of chopped curly parsley and chopped chives.

makes 8 or more skewers

2 skinless chicken breast fillets
2 chicken thighs, bones and skin removed
1 tbsp light soy sauce
2 garlic cloves, crushed
½ tsp cayenne pepper
1 tsp finely chopped ginger
2 tbsp chopped curly parsley
2 tbsp chopped chives
½ tsp fine sea salt
1 tsp brown sugar
white of 1 egg, lightly beaten
1 tbsp rice powder or plain flour
groundnut or sunflower oil, for frying
Peanut Sauce or Soy Sauce with Chillies (page 159), to serve

Cut the chicken into cubes, then put these through a mincer or chop finely with a cleaver or large knife. In a bowl, mix the chicken well with the soy sauce, garlic, spices, parsley, chives, salt and sugar. Stir in the egg white and rice powder or flour, and knead to combine everything thoroughly.

Divide the mix into 16 or 24 portions. Roll each portion into a ball or a sausage shape. Arrange in one layer on a plate, cover with cling-film and chill for several hours or overnight. Up to this point, the satays can be prepared well in advance.

When ready to cook, heat about 120 ml / 4 fl oz of oil in a non-stick pan and fry the pieces in two or three batches for about 2 minutes each batch, turning them often, until they are just starting to colour. Leave to cool enough to handle, then put 2 or 3 on each of 8 metal or wooden skewers (soak the latter well in cold water first to prevent them burning).

Just before serving, grill the satays over charcoal, or on a well-preheated ridged griddle pan, or under a gas or electric grill, for about 2 minutes, so that they are nicely browned. Serve hot with Peanut Sauce or any other sauce of your choice.

fresh shiitake stuffed with vegetable

tartare *I first came across this idea of vegetable tartare in a Southeast Asian restaurant, but I am not sure whether it got its name because the dressing is like tartare sauce or because the whole thing resembles Russian salad. Made carefully at home and served on pan-fried fresh shiitake mushrooms, it is delicious. (Fortunately, the days of rubbery reconstituted dried shiitake are fast receding.) I like to serve this as a starter with a salad of rocket and orange segments.*

*There are two major varieties of **basil** commonly used in cooking. Both grow throughout the Old World tropics, and both are fragrant-leaved herbs, but the leaf colours and flavours are quite different. 'Ordinary' or sweet basil (O. basilicum) has fresh, rather floppy green leaves with a characteristic strong smell, somewhat rank but pleasant. The 'other' basil, often called holy or sacred basil (O. gratissimum or sanctum) has dark green, glossy leaves and Thai varieties have purplish stems. It is widely regarded in the East as a sacred or magical plant, though no one seems sure why. I suspect that the two basils are often confused, and most Asian languages don't make much distinction between them. Although botanically related, their flavours and aromas are different.*

Holy basil is used in Southeast Asian cooking in soups, and in most dishes cooked in banana-leaf parcels. In Thailand, especially, basil is added to soups and curries, particularly green curries, in the last few minutes of cooking. Either variety of basil can be used here.

for 4

225–350 g / 8–12 oz fresh
shiitake mushrooms
salt and pepper
2 small carrots (about 100 g / 4 oz),
peeled and diced
60 g / 2 oz diced celeriac
60 g / 2 oz fresh soya beans (if available)
or shelled young broad beans, peeled
2 garlic cloves, finely chopped
a handful of basil leaves,
roughly chopped
3 tbsp best olive oil
2 ripe tomatoes, skinned, deseeded
and chopped, for garnish

for the tartare sauce
1 tbsp mustard (Dijon or any mustard
of your choice)
a pinch of cayenne pepper
1 tbsp Worcestershire sauce
1 tbsp capers, drained and chopped
2 tbsp chopped cornichons or small
pickled cucumbers
3–4 tbsp best virgin olive oil

Discard the stalks of all the shiitake. Keep aside 8 large shiitake, and dice the remainder.

Make the tartare sauce by mixing the ingredients in a small glass bowl, adding the olive oil last and stirring and mixing the sauce with a spoon or a small hand-beater. Set aside.

Put about 300 ml / ½ pint of water in a saucepan, add a large pinch of salt and bring to the boil. Add the carrots and cook them for 1 minute, then add the celeriac, the beans and the rest of the shiitake. Cover the pan for 2 minutes, then pour all the vegetables into a sieve and drain thoroughly. Leave to cool.

When cold, combine the vegetables with the tartare sauce. Mix them well, adding the garlic and basil. Then add salt and pepper to taste. Set aside.

Shortly before you plan to serve, heat the olive oil in a non-stick frying pan and fry the 8 whole shiitake for 2 minutes, then turn them over and cook for 1 minute more. Leave them to cool.

Heap the vegetable tartare on top of the cooked shiitake, shaping and pressing it firm with a spoon or a spatula. If some is left over, scatter it around the shiitake when you serve them. Sprinkle the chopped tomatoes over the shiitake as a garnish and serve at room temperature, with the salad suggested above or with any other salad of choice.

deep-fried breadfruit with a piquant Vietnamese dip

*From the cook's point of view, **breadfruit** (Artocarpus communis) is really more a vegetable than a fruit. It can be cooked in many different ways – usually cut into thick slices and either boiled, baked, or dried and baked as a kind of biscuit – but is never eaten raw. The following is a good way to cook it as a snack. It won't get very crisp, but the attraction lies in the tenderness and flavour inside the fried wedges. A family favourite in Asia, this treat has recently become quite common in restaurants as the gourmet market rediscovers its great appeal. A good alternative to the Vietnamese dip is guacamole, which can be bought ready-made.*

for 8-10

vegetable oil, for deep-frying
2 breadfruit, peeled, cut in half lengthwise and then each half cut into 6 slices
Piquant Vietnamese Dip (page 158)

Heat the oil (at least 600 ml / 1 pint) in a wok or deep-fryer (see page 63) and fry the breadfruit slices, 4–6 at a time, for 4–5 minutes per batch, or until golden brown. Take them out with a slotted spoon and drain on kitchen paper. Repeat, until all the slices have been fried.

Serve hot, warm or cold as snacks or canapés. Serve the dip in several small bowls, so everyone has their own, or at any rate is within easy reach of one.

sticky rice dumplings with a surprise filling

Here I was inspired by an Indian homemade cheese stuffing. The cheese is the Indian paneer, and the filling of paneer and green chillies I learned to make in New Delhi ten years ago was intended to stuff fresh morels, which in turn were destined to be cooked in that great Indian festive dish, a biryani. I was deeply impressed by the combination of soft cheese and chillies, which is unexpectedly delicious; so is this new recipe of mine.

makes 20-24

275 g / 10 oz glutinous rice flour
70 g / 2½ oz vegetable shortening

for the filling
115–175 g / 4–6 oz paneer, ricotta or other curd cheese
1–2 large green chillies, deseeded and finely chopped
½ tsp ground cumin
2 tsp finely chopped mint
1 tbsp raisins, soaked in hot water for 5 minutes, then drained and chopped
salt and freshly ground white pepper

First make the filling: in a glass bowl, mix all the ingredients together with a pinch of salt and several turns of the white peppermill. Set aside.

To make the glutinous rice dough, combine the flour and shortening with 300 ml / ½ pint of cold water. Knead this mixture until it becomes a soft dough. Roll a piece of dough into a ball the size of a walnut. Put this on a flat surface and flatten it with the palm of your hand. Put half a teaspoonful of filling in the centre, then roll the dough around the filling to make a round dumpling with the cheese filling inside it. Repeat until all the dough and filling are used up.

Fill a saucepan three-quarters full of water and bring it to the boil. Add half a teaspoonful of salt. Put 4–6 dumplings into the water and boil for 6–7 minutes or until they float to the surface. Repeat until all the dumplings are cooked.

Eat the dumplings hot or warm, whatever way you like them. In soup? Or with lightly salted, freshly grated coconut, or a dipping sauce?

lightly spiced cashew nuts

My garlicky peanuts, the recipe for which I've given (under different titles) in two of my previous books, are becoming very popular. You simply soak the nuts in boiling water containing crushed garlic and salt for 35–45 minutes, then deep-fry them until golden brown. I use the same method here for cashews, but with more spices. As well as making a great snack to serve with drinks, they may also be used as a flavouring or garnish, especially with poultry and fish.

for 8-10

500 g / 1 lb 2 oz shelled cashew nuts
about 1 litre / 2 pt boiling water
2 garlic cloves, crushed
2 tsp salt
2 tsp ground coriander seeds
½ tsp cayenne pepper
a large pinch of ground turmeric
sunflower or groundnut oil, for deep-frying

Put the nuts in a heatproof bowl and cover them with the boiling water. Add the garlic, salt and spices, and stir well to mix. Cover the bowl with a plate and leave the nuts to soak up the flavourings for 30 minutes. Drain the nuts in a colander and pat them dry with kitchen paper.

Heat the oil in a wok and fry the nuts in two batches for about 4 minutes each batch, stirring often. The nuts should be just slightly brown. Scoop them out and drain on kitchen paper.

Leave the nuts to get cold before storing in an airtight container in a dry place (don't refrigerate). They'll keep fresh and crunchy for at least 3–4 days.

mung bean crisps

I don't think you can find a more delicious crisp than these Indonesian rempeyek. You need to go to Oriental shops to get really fine rice powder, as the rice flour sold in most supermarkets is not fine enough. I specify rice powder because the finest possible grind is required. It used to be possible to find flour and powder, correctly labelled, in supermarkets as well as in Oriental shops. Unfortunately, anything labelled in the UK is now called 'rice flour', so an important distinction has been lost. Imported rice flour and powder, however, are still correctly labelled. To be sure of getting powder, look for imported product. If the recipe says 'rice flour', you can use rice powder; but if it says 'rice powder', it really means it. Instead of mung beans, you can also use halved peanuts.

for 8-10 (makes 60-70)

115 g / 4 oz mung beans,
soaked overnight in cold water
2 candlenuts
1 garlic clove
2 tsp ground coriander
1 tsp salt
115 g / 4 oz rice powder
groundnut or sunflower oil, for frying

Pound the nuts and garlic together, or process until smooth with 4 tablespoons of water. Transfer to a bowl, then add the coriander and salt. Mix in the rice powder with 225 ml / 8 fl oz cold water (or 150 ml / ¼ pint if you've already added water), a little at a time. Add the drained beans to this batter.

Heat about 1 cm / ½ inch of oil in a frying pan. Take 1 tablespoonful of batter, with some beans in it, and pour it into the pan so that it forms a flat shape. Go on spooning batter in, keeping the crisps separate as far as possible, until the pan is full. (In a 25 cm / 10 inch pan, you will probably be able to fry 10–12 small ones at a time.) Fry until set, 1–2 minutes. Lift out with a slotted spoon and drain on kitchen paper. Repeat until the batter is all used up.

In a deep-fryer or wok, heat oil to deep-fry the *rempeyek* (see page 63) and cook in several batches, until crisp and golden – each batch will take 1–2 minutes, depending on how hot the oil is. Lift out and drain on absorbent paper.

Leave the *rempeyek* to get cold, then store them in an airtight container. In the container, they will stay crisp for up to 2 weeks.

tofu and asparagus soufflé

A soufflé is not the first thing that comes to mind when you want to cook Southeast Asian food. However, tofu makes an excellent basis for a soufflé (as it does for ice-cream). I created this recipe as long ago as 1990, after Marie-Pierre Moine asked me to write some cutting-edge Asian recipes for Taste *magazine. Aptly, her article that accompanied my recipes was entitled 'Fast Forward'. The magazine no longer exists, but I think this recipe is still appropriate for a book on New wave Asian cooking. It uses smoked tofu, which was available in most large supermarkets even in those far-off days of 1990.*

for 4

60 g / 2 oz butter, plus more for greasing
30 g / 1 oz plain flour,
plus more for dusting
225 g / 8 oz asparagus, trimmed
salt and pepper
115 g / 4 oz smoked tofu
280 ml / ½ pt milk
a pinch of ground coriander
3 large eggs, separated

Preheat the oven to 200ºC / 400ºF / Gas 6 and generously butter and flour a medium soufflé dish or 4 large ramekins.

Cut 8 of the asparagus tips into 5 cm / 2 inch lengths. Boil the rest of the asparagus in 150 ml / ¼ pint of salted water for 4–5 minutes, until just tender. Drain well and set aside to cool.

Put the cooled asparagus in a blender, blend until smooth and rub through a sieve. Now blend the smoked tofu until smooth and set aside. Boil the reserved asparagus tips for 2–3 minutes and keep them for garnishing the soufflé.

Bring half of the milk with the butter almost to the boil in a saucepan. Lower the heat and season with salt, pepper and coriander. In a bowl, beat the egg yolks, then stir in the flour and mix in the remaining milk. Gradually add this mixture to the hot milk, whipping lightly all the time until the mixture thickens. Remove from the heat and stir in the sieved asparagus and smooth tofu.

Whisk the egg whites until stiff and lightly fold them into the mixture. Spoon the mixture into the prepared soufflé dish or ramekins and place the reserved asparagus tips on top.

Line a baking tray with a folded tea towel or newspaper and place the dish or ramekins on the tray. Pour in boiling water until it comes halfway up the sides of the dish or ramekins and cook in the oven for 15–20 minutes, until just set but still with a bit of wobble in the middle. Serve hot.

spiced potato croquettes
These croquettes are a nice way to spice up a traditional Western favourite. They don't need to be over-spiced, but a little chilli and ginger, along with a few chosen herbs, will make them special. Guests will enjoy them as canapés with drinks and the family will relish them as a change from more conventional ways of cooking potatoes – even chips. The easiest and quickest way to mash the potatoes is to use a potato ricer.

makes 20 small croquettes for canapés, or 12 larger ones to be eaten as snacks or to be served with a main course for 3-4

about 500 g / 1 lb or potatoes, preferably Desirée or King Edward, quartered

salt and pepper

4 eggs

60 g / 2 oz rice flour, plain flour or breadcrumbs

vegetable or groundnut oil, for deep-frying

for the spice and herb mixture

3 tbsp vegetable oil

4 shallots, thinly sliced

2 tsp finely chopped ginger

1 tsp chilli flakes or 2 fresh chillies, chopped

1 tsp roasted coriander seeds, roughly crushed in a mortar

2 tbsp chopped parsley

2 kaffir lime leaves, finely shredded, or a handful of mint leaves, chopped

1 tbsp rice flour or plain flour

Cook the potatoes in plenty of boiling salted water for 15–18 minutes, until they are quite tender. While they are cooking, hard-boil 2 of the eggs (i.e. cook for 8–10 minutes) and leave to cool.

While the potatoes and eggs are cooking, prepare the spice mixture: heat the oil in a wok or small pan and fry all the remaining ingredients except the flour, until the shallots begin to change colour. Continue stir-frying for 2 more minutes. Season with salt and pepper and leave the mixture to cool.

Drain the cooked potatoes in a colander. Put a few potato pieces at a time into a potato ricer while they are still hot and mash them into a bowl until all are mashed. (If you don't have a ricer, mash them thoroughly with a fork.)

When the spice mixture is cool, stir it well into the mashed potatoes and continue mixing and mashing with a fork. Shell the boiled eggs and chop them; separate the other 2 eggs and beat both the whites and the yolks lightly. Add the beaten egg yolks, chopped hard-boiled eggs and flour to the potatoes, and continue mixing, preferably by hand now, as the mixture should also be kneaded gently. Divide the mix into as many croquettes as you require and roll each croquette on greaseproof paper to make whatever shape you want – usually round or sausage-shaped. Chill them on a flat surface in the fridge until you are ready to fry them.

Heat about 600 ml / 1 pint of vegetable oil in a wok or deep-fryer. Dip each croquette in the egg white and roll it in flour or breadcrumbs. Deep-fry the croquettes in batches of 3–4 until they are golden brown. Drain on kitchen paper and serve hot or warm, as described above.

steamed aubergines with chillied garlic

I am very choosy about the aubergines I use for this dish. The familiar pear-shaped ones with purple-black glossy skins are not ideal. The right ones are the large round pale-purple aubergines, which are by no means impossible to find in most places but which are, I must admit, not always easily available. They have lovely thick flesh which becomes so juicy when they are cooked whole – either baked in the oven or steamed. If you suspect that this dish originated in China, then you are probably right, although this version uses coconut milk instead of soy sauce.

for 4

**2 large round purple aubergines,
each about 450 g / 1 lb
a little vegetable or olive oil,
for brushing (optional)**

**for the chillied garlic
10–12 garlic cloves
2 tbsp groundnut oil
2 bird's-eye chillies, deseeded
and finely chopped
1 large red chilli, deseeded
and finely chopped
1 tbsp ground almonds
1 tbsp fish sauce (nam pla)
115 ml / 4 fl oz thick coconut milk
(page 179)
juice of 1 lemon or lime
½ tsp salt
½ tsp brown sugar
a handful of pea shoots (page 22)
or watercress tips**

Steam the aubergines in a double saucepan or steam oven for 30–35 minutes; alternatively, bake in an oven preheated to 180ºC / 350ºF / Gas 4 for the same time. If they are to be baked, the aubergines must first be brushed or rubbed with some oil.

Prepare the chillied garlic: peel the garlic cloves and boil them in a small pan of water for 3 minutes. Drain. Heat the oil in another small pan and fry the chopped chillies and the garlic, mushing the garlic with a wooden spoon and stirring everything well, for about 2 minutes. Stir in the ground almonds, fish sauce and coconut milk. Bring to the boil and simmer for 4 minutes. Add the lemon or lime juice, salt and sugar. Stir and season with salt if necessary. Take off the heat.

To serve, cut the hot cooked aubergines in halves, then cut each half into 4–6 segments. Arrange on a large plate. Reheat the sauce for a minute or two, and, when hot, add the pea shoots or watercress tips just to wilt them. Pour over the aubergine segments and serve hot or warm.

grilled aubergines with avocado and tomato topping
The best aubergines for this are the long green Asian ones (pages 46–7), as they can be cut into slices of roughly the same size. Serve these as canapés with drinks, or as a starter with Avocado, Orange and Beetroot Salad (page 120).

serves 4-6

**2 long green aubergines, each sliced into
8 rounds, or 8 baby purple aubergines,
halved lengthwise
2 tbsp groundnut, sunflower or olive oil
¼ tsp cayenne pepper
¼ tsp salt
1 ripe avocado
2 red plum or vine tomatoes, skinned**

**for the marinade
juice of 1 lemon
1 tsp caster sugar
2 tsp fish sauce (nam pla)
or light soy sauce
1 garlic clove, crushed
2 tbsp chopped coriander or flat-leaf parsley
a pinch of chilli flakes**

As this is to be served cold, you can prepare everything well in advance. First, brush the aubergine slices or halves with a mixture of the oil, cayenne pepper and salt. Grill the aubergine pieces over or under an electric grill, or on a ridged griddle pan (in batches if necessary). They need to be well cooked, so keep an eye on them; you may have to turn them several times. The whole process will take 8–10 minutes for each batch. Set the cooked pieces aside, in a single layer, until ready to serve.

Make the marinade by mixing the ingredients in a glass bowl. Peel the avocado and cut it up either in small slices or in cubes. Put the cut pieces straight into the marinade to prevent discoloration. Cut up the tomatoes the same way you did the avocado and add these to the marinade. Time the operation so that avocado and tomatoes are in the marinade for not longer than 10 minutes. Then drain them well.

Arrange the avocado and tomato pieces on top of the cooked aubergine pieces, and serve as suggested above.

aubergine variety

Everyone is familiar with the enormous shiny **purple aubergines (*Solanum melongena*)** that look like tubby Zeppelins, but these are, so to speak, the tip of the aubergine iceberg. Aubergines, originally called egg-plants by English gardeners who grew them as exotic ornaments (and this is still what they are called in the USA), can be found in Southeast Asia in many shapes, sizes and colours.

The smallest are **pea aubergines (*S. torvum*)**, which are actually about the size of large peas or small cherries. Other aubergines, which are nearly all cultivars of *S. melongena*, may be globular, flattened globes, egg-shaped, or more or less club-shaped. In colour they can be white, green, yellow or purple, with shades ranging from light to intense, and with whites and greens often fading delicately into each other. These last are often called apple aubergines.

Chinese white and **Chinese green varieties** are long and fairly straight, narrow at the stem end, then broadening a little towards the tip. *S. ferox* (not shown here) is a small, hairy fruit produced on a very prickly plant; it is extremely bitter and is said to be eaten as a relish with curries in India, Thailand and Malaysia.

One of my favourite aubergine varieties is 'Violet Pearl', now sold in many supermarkets, because they are thin-skinned and have soft flesh. I either steam or roast them, then cut them into wedges. Just before serving, I pour over them some Sambal Goreng Sauce (page 162) and stir in the juice of a lemon.

All aubergines contain about 6% carbohydrates, and 1% protein.

❶ purple aubergines (sizes vary considerably);
❷ an assortment of different types and colours of aubergine, with pea aubergines in the foreground and small purple aubergines, often sold as 'baby aubergines' at the top left.

fried dishes

We do a tremendous amount of frying in Southeast Asia. There may be lots of reasons for this, to do with the fuels and cooking media traditionally used, but the fact certainly is that we like fried food. Frying – especially deep-frying – is quick, you can usually see at once when the food is cooked, and it produces the most delicious crunchy textures and flavours that you can really get your teeth into. Finally, done with skill and understanding, frying is healthier than it's sometimes given credit for, as food fried properly – particularly in deep-frying – absorbs very little oil. If you want your meal to follow a traditional Southeast Asian pattern, then all the principal methods of cooking should be represented: one or more steamed dishes, dishes with sauce (that is, curries), fried or grilled dishes, and several dipping sauces and sambals. It's important that everyone present, even the hardest to please, should find at least one dish to their liking.

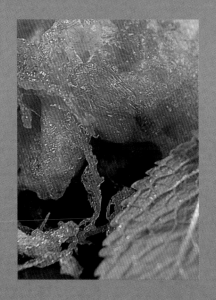

pan-fried cod with chillied anchovies

This is my new approach to cooking and presenting a cod fillet (though you can make it with other firm-fleshed white fish, such as halibut or haddock, with equally good results). Although this way of cooking fish with onions and chillies is typical of my homeland in West Sumatra, the finished dish is quite unlike anything that I ate when I was a child. It would normally have been deep-fried or barbecued, there would have been many more chillies and the anchovies used would be dried ones. You can eat the dish with chips and salad by all means, if you wish, but I personally would serve it with fried rice (page 150) or fried noodles.

for 4 as a main course

4 cod fillets, each weighing about 115–150 g / 4–5 oz, with or without skin
1 tbsp lime juice
1 tbsp demerara sugar
½ tsp salt
2 tbsp vegetable oil

for the chillied anchovies
3–4 tbsp vegetable oil
4–6 shallots, thinly sliced
2 tsp finely chopped ginger
2–4 large red chillies, deseeded and thinly sliced
6–8 canned anchovies in oil, drained and chopped

Rub the cod fillets with lime juice, sugar and salt, then leave them in a cool place for an hour or so.

Preheat the oven to 190ºC / 375ºF / Gas 5. Prepare the chillied anchovies: heat the oil in a wok and stir-fry the shallots, ginger and chillies for about 4 minutes. Drain, reserving the oil. Put the shallots, ginger and chillies back into the wok and add the chopped anchovies. Set aside.

Heat the oil for the fish, together with the oil reserved from frying the shallots, in a non-stick frying pan. Arrange the cod fillets side by side in the pan and cook for 2 minutes. Turn over and cook on the other side for 2 minutes. Turn off the heat and transfer the fillets to the preheated oven for 2–4 minutes.

When ready to serve, transfer the fish to a warmed serving platter. Heat the mixture in the wok, stirring gently, for 1 minute. Then spread the mix over the cod fillets. Serve hot, as described above.

salted cod dumplings

I'm using home-salted cod here, and for that you really need to allow 24 hours for the fish to be salted properly. It's not really practical to salt less than a kilogram, so I would suggest you make this for a largish drinks party. However, salted cod can be kept in the fridge for up to 3 days and there are plenty of other things you can do with it. These dumplings are my version of the starchy fish balls or fish cakes that are sold in so many Oriental supermarkets. A lot of these are bought by Oriental restaurants to put into soups, noodle dishes and stir-fries, but mine are meant to be served as canapés on cucumber slices, or as a starter on Cos lettuce leaves garnished with Coconut Sambal.

about 1–1.5 kg / 2–3 lb skinless cod fillet
85–115 g / 3–4 oz coarse sea salt
2 tbsp finely chopped parsley (curly or flat)
2 tsp finely chopped lemon grass
(soft inner part only)
1 tsp fine sea salt
¼ tsp palm sugar or brown sugar
2 tsp cornflour, dissolved in 2 tbsp water
whites of 2 eggs
groundnut or sunflower oil, for frying
cucumber slices or Cos lettuce leaves,
to serve
Coconut Sambal (page 160), to garnish

for the spice mixture
2 shallots, chopped
2 candlenuts or macadamia nuts
or 4 blanched almonds, chopped
1–4 green bird's-eye chillies, chopped
2 garlic cloves, chopped
1 tsp chopped ginger
2 tsp roasted coriander seeds, crushed
2 tsp lemon juice
2 tbsp vegetable oil

Salt the cod 24 hours before making the dumplings: coat the fish well with the salt, rubbing it all over. Lay the fish flat in a glass or ceramic container, cover with cling-film, and keep in the fridge for 24 hours.

Next day, rinse the fish under cold running water and then soak it in cold water for 30 minutes. Drain and pat dry with kitchen paper. (You can now refrigerate it, if necessary, for up to 3 days before cooking it.)

Make the spice mixture by blending all the ingredients until smooth. Transfer the mix to a saucepan and simmer, stirring often, for 4–6 minutes. Leave to get cold.

Chop 450 g / 1 lb of the salted cod finely. In a glass bowl, mix it well with the parsley, lemon grass, salt, sugar and the cold spice mixture. Add the cornflour mixture and egg whites. Stir this mixture with a wooden spoon, in one direction only, until it has amalgamated and is becoming difficult to stir.

Form the mixture into several sausage shapes, about 2 cm / ¾ inch in diameter. Two-thirds fill a saucepan with water and bring to the boil. Put the sausages in and boil them for 2 minutes. Drain them, pat them dry and leave to cool.

When they are cold, cook them in a little oil in a non-stick frying pan, turning them often, until they are golden brown. Again leave them to get cold before slicing them into rounds about 1cm / ½ inch thick. Serve cold, as suggested above.

fried snapper and egg noodles with a coating of Parmesan and chilli *There are actually some Southeast Asian dishes that are cooked in wine and use dairy cream or cheese.*

for 2-3
225 g / 8 oz fine egg noodles
450 g / 1 lb red snapper fillets (ask your
fishmonger to scale the fish well)
2 tbsp plain flour or rice flour
about 1 tsp coarse sea salt
½ tsp cayenne pepper
4 tbsp freshly grated Parmesan cheese
2 tbsp chopped parsley
1 large red chilli, deseeded and finely chopped
1–2 egg(s), lightly beaten
groundnut or sunflower oil, for deep-frying
2 ripe tomatoes, skinned, deseeded
and cubed, to garnish

Pre-cook the noodles in a large pan of boiling water for 2–3 minutes, then refresh under cold running water. Wash the fish well in very cold water and then cut into pieces – whatever shape and size you wish. Pat dry with kitchen paper. On a flat plate, mix the flour, sea salt and cayenne pepper. Set aside.

When almost ready to serve, reheat the noodles by pouring boiling water over them from the kettle. Drain and transfer to a glass bowl. While they are still hot, toss in the Parmesan cheese, chopped parsley, chillies and salt to taste.

Coat the fish fillets in the egg, then roll in the flour. Heat the oil in a wok or deep-fryer (see page 63) and cook the fish in 2 or 3 batches for 2–3 minutes each. Drain on kitchen paper.

To serve: divide the dressed noodles among warmed serving plates. Arrange the fried fish on top and garnish with the tomato. A side dish of mixed salad in a piquant or French dressing makes a good accompaniment.

savoury banana and prawn paste fritters

If you can buy ripe plantains from your local supermarket or ethnic food shop, then use these instead of ordinary yellow bananas. In this very new wave pairing, the spiced prawn paste (more or less that used on traditional prawn toasts) will give the fritters some warmth and bite, to cut the sweetness of the plantains (or bananas). I like to make these fritters quite small, just a mouthful each, but if you want them larger – say, two bites – then cut the banana / plantain obliquely into ovals instead of plain rounds.

makes 16-18 round fritters or 12-14 oval ones

2 large ripe plantains or 4 slightly under-ripe bananas, sliced as above
groundnut or vegetable oil, for deep-frying
Soy Sauce with Chillies (page 159), to serve (optional)

for the prawn paste
225 g / 8 oz raw shelled prawns, without heads, chopped
2 tbsp chopped spring onions
2 garlic cloves, crushed
2–4 bird's-eye chillies, finely chopped
1 tbsp fish sauce (nam pla)
60 g / 2 oz minced pork fat (optional)
1 tsp chopped lemon grass (soft inner part only)
a large pinch of salt
1 tsp cornflour
white of 1 egg

for the batter
115 g / 4 oz rice powder or plain flour
115 ml / 4 fl oz cold water
1 tsp ground coriander
2 garlic cloves, crushed
1 tsp salt
1 tbsp groundnut oil or clarified butter

Make the prawn paste by putting all the ingredients into a blender and blending until smooth. Chill for at least 30 minutes.

Meanwhile, make the batter by mixing the ingredients in another glass bowl.

Spread a heaped teaspoonful of prawn paste on top of a slice of plantain or banana, then put another slice on top of the filling to make a sandwich. Repeat this process until all the slices and filling are used up. (If you have a little paste left over, you can spread it on small slices of day-old bread, then fry these, without batter, to make prawn toast.)

Heat the oil in a wok or deep-fryer (see page 63). When hot, dip the sandwiches in the batter and deep-fry them, 4 or 5 at a time, for 2–3 minutes. Scoop them out with a slotted spoon and drain on layers of kitchen paper. Continue frying until all are done.

Serve hot or warm, as canapés with drinks. Dipping sauce is optional, but I recommend Soy Sauce with Chillies.

prawn and sweet potato cakes *This is another*
of Southeast Asia's most popular snacks – deep-fried, of course. If deep-frying is not
your style of cooking, these sweet potato cakes can be shallow-fried in a non-stick
frying pan. **Sweet potatoes** *(Ipomoea batatas, illustrated on pages 14–15) sold in*
the West are usually orange-fleshed, but there are white varieties. The yellow varieties
contain carotene, which turns them yellow and provides some vitamin A, so these
are more nutritious as well as more appealing to the eye. If you see these cakes in
an Asian food market, but they are purple instead of white or orange, then you know
they have been made with taro (page 15).

Sweet potato is one of the root-tubers that are widely grown in the tropics, particularly
in drier areas, as a starchy staple or filling snack. It is in fact the most important of them,
and is still preferred to rice in some areas. Names often get confused, and the Indonesian
word ketela *is often applied to cassava (pages 13 and 15), which in turn is sometimes*
called sweet potato in English; the word yam is used for these and at least one other
food tuber. Although botanically the three plants are unrelated, it has to be said that
from the cooking and eating point of view they do look and taste very similar.

makes about 20

2 sweet potatoes, weighing about
350 g / 12 oz

salt

28–30 raw prawns, shells
and heads removed

4 tbsp chopped spring onions or chives

for the batter

2 tbsp rice flour or plain flour

1 tsp cornflour

¼ tsp salt

¼ tsp freshly ground black pepper

1 tsp baking powder

Slice the sweet potatoes into thin rounds, then cut these into tiny sticks. Put the sticks in a bowl of slightly salted cold water. Keep them in the water until you are ready to mix them with the batter.

To make the batter: sift the flours, salt, pepper and baking powder into a bowl. Pour in 4 tablespoons of cold water, a little at a time, while whisking the batter with a fork. The batter needs to have the consistency of thick pouring cream. Taste, and add more salt if necessary.

Reserving 20 whole, finely chop the remaining prawns. Drain the sweet potato sticks and dry them with kitchen paper. Mix them into the batter, together with the chopped prawns and spring onions or chives. Mix well.

Heat the oil in a wok or deep-fryer. Form the prawn and sweet potato cakes by putting a spoonful of the mixture from the bowl on a small plate, then pressing a whole prawn into the middle of it. Arrange up to 4 cakes in the deep-fryer basket and submerge them in the hot oil for 2–3 minutes. Take them out and drain them on layers of kitchen paper. (Alternatively, deep-fry 4 at a time in hot oil in a wok, turning them over once after about 1½ minutes. The whole cooking time should be about 3 minutes per batch. If you shallow-fry the cakes in a non-stick pan, you will need to turn them over several times but the total cooking time will be the same.)

Serve the cakes hot, warm or cold, as snacks. They also make excellent starters, if you allow 2–3 cakes per person, arranged on a bed of well-dressed green salad.

minced prawn and tofu cake
I still meet people who tell me that tofu is tasteless and they don't like the texture. Being such a lover of tofu myself, however, I know that their complaints are totally unfounded and that all I have to do is demonstrate to them that tofu is not only stuffed full of protein but absolutely delicious as well. There is a lot of it in this book, always artfully combined with other ingredients. This recipe, for example, is very simple to make and you can spice it up even more with a hot dipping sauce, like Mild Curry Sauce (page 163), or guacamole.

makes about 20-24 canapés

225 g / 8 oz raw shelled prawns, without heads

225 g / 8 oz firm tofu (Japanese or Chinese), chopped and excess water squeezed out

2 tbsp rice flour or plain flour

1 tsp baking powder

2 tbsp strong tamarind water (page 164) or lemon juice

2 eggs, lightly beaten

groundnut or sunflower oil, for frying

for the flavouring mixture

4–6 shallots, finely chopped

4 garlic cloves, finely chopped

2 tsp finely chopped ginger

2 tbsp chopped chives or green onions

1 tsp finely chopped rosemary

2–4 bird's-eye chillies, chopped

2 kaffir lime leaves, finely shredded (optional)

1 tsp salt

2 tsp ground coriander seeds

First make the flavouring mixture: in a wok, stir-fry all the ingredients until the shallots start to brown. Transfer to a bowl and leave to cool.

Add the prawns and tofu to the cooled mixture, mixing them in well with a fork. Add the flour, baking powder, tamarind water or lemon juice and the beaten eggs. Knead all these into a paste with your hands. Taste it and add more salt if required.

When ready to serve, heat some oil in a non-stick frying pan. Scoop up a dessertspoonful of the mixture and drop it into the hot oil. Keep doing this until there are 6–8 scoops of the mix in the pan. Cook for 2 minutes, then turn them over. Cook for another 2 minutes, then take them out and drain on kitchen paper. Repeat until all the mixture has been fried.

Serve as described above, hot, warm or cold.

deep-fried rice paper prawn rolls

These are the traditional 'spring rolls' of Vietnam, cha gio tom. They are another example of snacks that are good to eat wrapped in a lettuce leaf with a few mint leaves, then dipped in nuoc cham (fish sauce with chillies and grated carrots). However, the filling has plenty of flavour and the rolls can be served as canapés without lettuce leaves or dipping sauce. Vietnamese rice paper (banh trang) is trickier to handle than the Chinese spring roll wrappers that can be found in the freezers of Oriental food stores. For fried spring rolls I would use either, but for fresh rolls rice paper really is necessary. For more on wrappers, see page 145.

makes 20-24 small rolls

20–24 rice paper discs or triangles, about 18 cm / 7½ in across (allow a few extra in case some are torn)
vegetable oil, for deep-frying

for the filling
225 g / 8 oz minced pork
115–175 g / 4–6 oz raw prawns, shells and heads removed, deveined, then chopped
4 shallots, finely chopped
3 garlic cloves, finely chopped
4 tbsp finely chopped spring onions
30 g / 1 oz glass vermicelli, soaked for 10 minutes in hot (not boiling) water, drained, then cut into pieces about 2.5 cm / 1 in long
6–8 fresh shiitake mushrooms, stalks removed and thinly sliced
60 g / 2 oz mangetout, sliced thinly at an angle
2 tbsp fish sauce (nuoc mam, page 164)
1 tbsp light soy sauce
¼ tsp freshly ground black pepper
1 egg

Make the filling by mixing all the ingredients in a glass bowl. If the filling is to remain uncooked, add the egg now. If you want to pre-cook the filling, do not put the egg in yet. In either case, mix well.

Provided your glass bowl is microwave-proof, heat the mixture in the bowl in a microwave oven at full power for 1½ minutes. Alternatively, transfer the filling to a non-stick saucepan, set it on medium heat and stir for about 3 minutes. Whichever method you use, don't add the egg until the filling is cold.

When you are ready to start frying and not before, start filling and rolling your rice-paper discs. Have a flat plate or tray in front of you. Put a bowl of cold water on one side of it and the bowl of filling on the other. Dip the rice-paper discs one at a time into the water, leaving each disc in the water for 10 seconds only. Lift the disc out, spread it on a damp tea towel, and immediately pat it with kitchen paper. The rice paper will now be pliable.

Lift up the edge of the disc at the point that is nearest you and fold it away from you to make a fold about 3 cm / 1 inch wide. On top of this fold, arrange a tablespoonful of filling. Pick up the straight edge of the fold and roll it one full turn away from you, making a tube with the filling inside. Now fold the left- and right-hand edges of the disc inwards to shut the ends of the tube. Then continue rolling until you get to the far side of the disc. Continue filling and rolling until all the ingredients have been used up. As you finish each roll, lay it on a tray or plate, seam downwards. Make sure the rolls do not touch each other – if they do, they will cling.

To be really crisp, these rolls need to be fried twice. Heat the oil in a wok or deep-fryer (see page 63) and fry 4 or 5 rolls at a time for 3–4 minutes. They are liable still to cling to each other until they have been frying for at least 2 minutes. Stir them around until they begin to change colour, then scoop them out with a slotted spoon or wire scoop. Drain on kitchen paper. Continue this process until all the rolls have been fried once.

You can proceed to the second frying straight away, or the rolls can be refrigerated for up to 48 hours. If you refrigerate them, make sure they come out of the fridge with enough time to warm up to room temperature before the second frying. The second frying lasts 2–3 minutes, which should make the rolls golden brown and crisp.

Serve the rolls hot; they should stay crisp at room temperature for at least an hour.

deep-fried squid in rice powder batter

*For the batter, anything actually labelled 'rice flour' is almost certainly too coarse;
it is essential to use the finest 'rice powder' from an Oriental food shop (see page 41).
Buy small squid that can be cut into rings. The batter has a good flavour already, and
a dipping sauce is really not necessary, unless you want a hot chilli sauce. The addition
of the candlenuts adds richness to the batter and helps hold it together. Like a new
wave version of traditional calamari, these squid rings will be excellent with noodles
or pasta dressed with the Red Pepper and Tomato Sauce on page 163.*

**for 4 as a starter or 2 as
a main course with
noodles or pasta**

**450–675 g / 1–1½ lb cleaned small
squid without tentacles, cut into
rings about 5 mm / ¼ in thick
1 tbsp lemon juice
½ tsp salt
½ tsp cayenne pepper
groundnut or vegetable oil, for frying**

**for the batter
2 candlenuts or macadamia
nuts, chopped
2 garlic cloves, chopped
115 g / 4 oz rice powder
2 tsp ground coriander
1 tsp salt**

In a glass bowl, rub the squid rings with lemon juice, salt and cayenne pepper. Set aside.

Make the batter: put the chopped nuts, garlic and 4 tablespoons of cold water in a blender and blend until smooth. Transfer to a glass bowl and add the rice powder, coriander, salt and 115 ml / 4 fl oz more water. Stir vigorously with a spoon (an advantage of rice powder is that it always makes a smooth batter). However, you will need to stir the batter every time before you take out each spoonful of squid, otherwise the batter at the bottom of the bowl will be much thicker than that at the top.

Heat the oil for deep-frying in a wok or deep-fryer (see page 63). Put half the squid rings into the batter and move them around so the batter coats the squid well. Put them into the hot oil, a few at a time, and fry for 1–2 minutes only, then take them out with a perforated spoon and drain on kitchen paper. Fry the rest in the same way.

Serve them hot or warm, as a snack or hot canapé, as a starter with a salad, or with pasta as described above.

pan-fried scallops with fried wonton
parcels *In Southeast Asia, those who eat scallops at all will simply steam
them briefly. Fried wontons, with a filling of your own choice (see page 145), are
popular everywhere. Serving these two items together as a starter will accentuate their
contrasting textures and sharpen your appetite for the next course. My choice here
for the wonton filling is prawn paste used in my recipe for Savoury Banana and Prawn
Paste Fritters on page 52, and I would serve these with Soy Sauce with Chillies (page
159), or just with Asinan Jakarta (page 122).*

8 scallops, with or without corals,
each cut into 2 round slices
1 tbsp lemon juice
a large pinch of salt
8–12 wonton skins
Prawn paste made from 125 g / 4 oz
prawns (page 52)
white of 1 egg, lightly beaten
8–12 Chinese chive stalks (optional)
groundnut or sunflower oil, for frying
and deep-frying

Rub the scallops with lemon juice and salt, and set aside in a cool place.

To fill the wontons: lay 4 wonton skins side by side on a flat surface. Put a teaspoonful of prawn paste in the centre of each. Brush a circle of egg white on the surface around the filling. Gather up the 4 sides of the wonton and squeeze together so that the egg white makes them stick; now you have a little bag with the filling inside. If you want it to look prettier, tie a bow around it with a Chinese chive. Do this until you have filled all the wonton skins.

When ready to serve, put 2 tablespoonfuls of the oil in a non-stick frying pan and pan-fry the scallop slices for 2 minutes over a high heat, turning once. In a small saucepan or wok, heat enough oil to deep-fry the wontons and fry them, 4 at a time, until golden brown and crisp (2–3 minutes for each batch).

Filipino fried stuffed duck *Spanish influence is seen here in*

the ingredients of the stuffing. The methods of cooking, on the other hand, are reminiscent of China: steaming the duck first to cook it through, then deep-frying it in a wok to crisp the skin. You can, in fact, do both in some modern ovens, which combine steam cooking and hot air (though I think not both at once). Here the duck has been boned. This is not traditional anywhere in Southeast Asia, where we enjoy picking every shred of meat from every bone, but I know that many people in the West prefer not to have to bother with this. To remove the bones of the carcass, cut along the back of the duck, not along the breastbone. Afterwards, put in the stuffing, then sew the cut with needle and thread.

for 4 as a main course

1 duck, about 1.5–2 kg / 3½–4 lb
(boned as above, optional)
juice of 1 lemon
½ tsp salt
½ tsp freshly ground pepper
groundnut or sunflower oil, for deep-frying

for the stuffing

2 red onions, roughly chopped
3 tbsp groundnut oil or clarified butter
225 g / 8 oz chestnut mushrooms, sliced
115 g / 4 oz best Spanish cooked ham
(or other good cooked ham), cut into
1 cm / ½ in cubes
115 g / 4 oz tenderloin of pork
or belly of pork, minced
60 g / 2 oz fresh breadcrumbs
1 tsp salt
½ tsp cayenne pepper
2 tbsp chopped parsley
1 egg, lightly beaten

Rub the duck inside and out with the lemon juice, salt and pepper.

Make the stuffing: fry the onion in the oil until soft. Leave it to cool, then mix it with all the other ingredients except the egg, kneading them lightly. Finally add the egg and continue mixing and kneading for a minute or two longer. Put the stuffing into the body cavity of the duck and also into the neck. Truss the duck with string and steam for 60–70 minutes. Leave to get cold.

Pat the skin of the cooled duck dry with kitchen towels. Heat the oil in a wok until beginning to smoke. Carefully lower the duck into the hot oil, and cook it for 2 minutes. Turn it over and cook it for another 2 minutes on its other side. Give it a quarter-turn and cook another 2 minutes, then turn it again and cook a further 2 minutes. By turning the duck in this way, you will make its skin brown and crisp all over in 8–10 minutes. The flesh of the duck and the stuffing are, of course, already cooked. Lift the duck out of the oil, lay it on a tray or large plate lined with kitchen paper and leave it to drain well.

To serve, the boned duck can be cut across to make neat slices. Cut a duck still with bones lengthwise into two halves. Then cut each half across into two, leaving the stuffing undisturbed inside the pieces. Serve hot with rice, accompanied by stir-fried or braised vegetables such as cabbage, Chinese cabbage or beans.

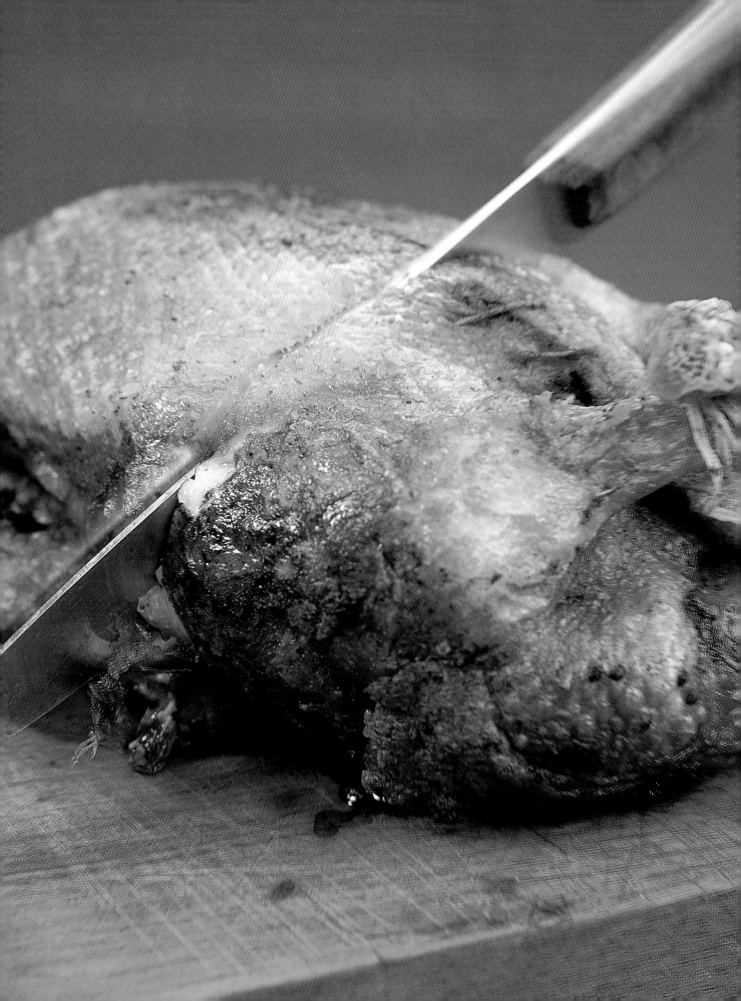

the principles of deep-frying

Perhaps surprisingly, deep-frying, done correctly, is a healthy way to cook, as the food absorbs very little oil. It also tastes delicious and has the textures that we associate with properly fried food – crisp on the outside and tender inside. Badly deep-fried, on the other hand, the food has the opposites vices: it becomes oily, soggy and tasteless, and it will not do you or your waistline any good.

Much is at stake, therefore, when you reach for the deep-fryer, or whatever pan you use for the job. With practice, you will get equally good results with an ordinary saucepan. A wok, though, is what we always used in the East when I was a girl, and I still do a lot of my deep-frying in a wok in London today.

The golden rules

There are two golden rules for deep-frying. First, you must have enough oil really to immerse whatever is being fried so that it all cooks at once and quickly. Shallow-frying is a different technique, for which you may often need to use the bare minimum of oil; deep-frying only works when you have plenty. If the recipe prescribes the amount, obey it. Many recipes, however, don't specify an exact quantity because pans and fryers vary so much in size and shape. As keeping the oil temperature steady is so important, it is obviously not a good idea to add too much food to the hot oil at a time, so deep-frying is usually best done in smallish batches.

The second rule is that the oil temperature must be right, within reasonable but not very broad limits; otherwise the food will absorb oil before its exterior crisps up. This is one big advantage of the deep-fryer, it is almost certain to have a thermostat to get the oil to the right heat and maintain it there for as long as you need it. If you use a pan or a wok, you will have to rely on experience and instinct to tell you how to control the heat. A kitchen thermometer is well worth having. Many cookbooks will tell you that a cube of stale bread thrown into oil at the right temperature will brown in 60 seconds. If you use the kitchen thermometer, then as a general rule the oil temperature should be at least 160°C/325°F and up to 180°–190°C/350–375°F.

Be careful!

The temperatures involved are considerably hotter than boiling water and this is obviously potentially hazardous if you are careless.

Also, remember if you are not using an automatic deep-fryer never to leave heating oil unattended as it will spontaneously ignite if allowed to get too hot – in other words, beyond its smoking point.

Cooking tempura prawns (page 21): **❶** spearing them on satay sticks for ease, dipping the prawns in the tempura batter to coat them, taking care to let any excess drip back into the bowl; **❸** immersing the coated prawns in the hot oil; **❹** don't deep-fry too much at a time, or the oil temperature will be too reduced to cook properly; **❺** remove the cooked prawns as soon as they are a good golden colour, and put to drain as **❷**.

bamboo shoot special fritters

There are endless varieties of fritters in Southeast Asia, because deep-frying is a very simple and widespread technique of cooking. This combination of pork stuffing and julienned bamboo shoots originated in Laos and is well known on the other side of the Mekong, in northern Thailand. I remember, years ago, in a food market in Chiang Mai, watching a young woman frying these fritters in an immense iron wok. There, they use only the tips of the young bamboo shoots, splitting them into fine strips from the cut end to just below the tip and then splaying these strips out like the ribs of a half-open umbrella to hold the pork stuffing. In the West, although you can quite often buy young bamboo shoots in cans or glass jars, I find it much simpler to use sliced bamboo shoots. Cut these into tiny sticks and put the stuffing between two layers of sticks, as described below.

makes about 16-18

500 g / about 1 lb canned sliced
bamboo shoots, drained, then
thoroughly rinsed
2–3 tbsp rice flour or plain flour
2 eggs
groundnut or sunflower oil,
for deep-frying
lettuce leaves, to serve (optional)
mint leaves, to serve (optional)
Peanut Sauce (page 159),
to serve (optional)

for the stuffing
175–225 g / 6–8 oz pork
tenderloin, minced
6 shallots, very finely chopped
4 tbsp finely chopped spring onions
or chives
1 tsp fish sauce (nam pla)
¼ tsp salt
½ tsp cayenne pepper
1 tbsp rice flour or plain flour

Make the stuffing by mixing all the ingredients in a bowl. Roll a small ball of the mixture, about as big as a walnut, and fry or grill this to taste the seasoning. Add more salt if necessary. Divide into 16–18 portions.

Dry the tiny sticks of bamboo shoot with kitchen paper. Lay a few on a flat surface. Place a portion of stuffing on top of them, and flatten the stuffing a little with the palm of your hand. Lay roughly the same number of bamboo shoot sticks on top of the stuffing, and again press lightly with your hand to make a kind of thick sandwich. Repeat, until all the bamboo sticks and stuffing are used.

Arrange the fritters in one layer on a plate that will fit your steamer, or on two plates if necessary. Steam, a plateful at a time, for 5–8 minutes. Leave to get cold.

When ready to start frying, sift the flour on to a flat plate. Beat the egg in a small bowl, adding a pinch of salt. Heat the oil for deep-frying in a wok (see page 63). Dip each fritter into the beaten egg, then roll it in flour. Fry the fritters, a few at a time, in the hot oil, turning them once or twice, for about 2 minutes or until they are nicely browned. Take them out with a slotted spoon and drain on kitchen paper. (Alternatively, fry the fritters in a deep-fryer until golden brown.)

Serve hot, warm or cold, as snacks or as a starter with lettuce leaves and mint. A good way to eat them is to lay a fritter on a lettuce leaf with 2 or 3 mint leaves, then roll up the leaf as a wrapper and dip it into Peanut sauce (page 159).

satays, grills and barbecues

Barbecuing is such a familiar occupation for warm summer evenings, especially in countries where summer does not last all the year round, that no home seems complete without its paraphernalia. In the tropics, where sundown is always around six o'clock and evenings generally dry and fresh, the barbecue cult has never really caught on, perhaps because we have been grilling our food over glowing charcoal for millennia. Only where tourists gather will you find that the barbecue has become forever fashionable. I know this because I no longer have to explain that satays are the same as kebabs. Whichever label is attached to these skewers loaded with marinated meat or vegetables, and regardless of how many empty skewers are sitting on the edge of people's plates when they've finished, an Asian will regard satays as a mere snack if they are not eaten with rice.

tuna and butternut squash satays

Butternut squash are so easy to get now and I have become so accustomed to cooking with them that I adapt any Asian pumpkin recipe to suit this good-tasting yellow American cousin. All Asians love tuna, which at the time of writing happens to be a fashion favourite, widely available as fresh tuna steaks. (Whether it is really fresh, or has been thawed from great frozen chunks of fish, I am not always quite sure.) These satays can be served as a starter with a green salad. As a main course, a good accompaniment would be fried rice (page 150), or a salad and some new potatoes.

**for 4 as a starter or
2 as a main course**

**2 tuna steaks, each 100–115 g /
3½–4 oz, each cut into 4 cubes
1 butternut squash weighing about 450 g /
1 lb, peeled, and cut into
thick cubes, about 2.5 cm
/ 1 in on a side
Soy Sauce with Chillies (page 159)
or Peanut Sauce (page 159),
to serve (optional)**

**for the marinade
juice of 1 lemon
2 tbsp light soy sauce
3 garlic cloves, crushed
1 tbsp very finely chopped ginger
1 tsp chilli flakes or coarsely
ground pepper
¼ tsp salt**

Well ahead, make the marinade by mixing the ingredients in a glass bowl. Add the pieces of tuna and squash and mix them well so that they are coated on all sides. Leave for 2 hours.

Heat a little oil in a non-stick frying pan and fry the butternut squash cubes until tender, about 5–7 minutes. Alternatively, put them on a plate and microwave on full power for 2 minutes. Leave to get cold.

Just before you are ready to serve, push alternating cubes of tuna and squash on to soaked bamboo skewers and grill for 1 minute on one side, then turn them over and grill for another minute on the other side. This will cook the tuna perfectly, and the squash only needs to be reheated.

Serve straight away, as suggested above. If you want a dipping sauce to add extra flavour and to moisten your satay, use Soy Sauce with Chillies or Peanut Sauce.

prawn and minced prawn satays

These attractive-looking satays will usually vanish before anything else if you serve them as part of the fare for a barbecue party, so be prepared for heavy demand. They are made with large whole prawns and smaller ones that are minced for the prawn paste; the ones that are to be cooked whole should, I suggest, have their tails left on for appearance's sake. They look better still in their whole shells, but it's quite a sticky-fingered business getting the shells off after they're grilled. The marinade works just as well with chicken, duck and pork, which you can put on skewers in a similar way to the prawns – thin slices of meat alternating with balls of the meat paste.

makes 8 skewers

32 large prawns, shelled and deveined, but the tails left on
450 g / 1 lb raw shelled small prawns
1 tsp cornflour, dissolved in
1 tbsp cold water
white of 1 egg
2 tbsp sesame seeds, dry-roasted until lightly coloured
2 tbsp rice flour or plain flour
juice of 1 lemon
2 tbsp groundnut or olive oil

for the marinade

1 tsp finely chopped fresh galingal (page 109)
1 tsp finely chopped lemon grass, soft inner part only
2 tbsp finely chopped coriander leaves and roots or stalks
4 spring onions, cut into thin rounds
2 garlic cloves, crushed
2 fresh or dried bird's-eye chillies, finely chopped
4 tbsp chopped or shaved creamed coconut (page 179), dissolved in
115 ml / 4 fl oz hot water
juice of 1 lime or lemon
1 tsp light soy sauce or fish sauce (nam pla)
½–1 tsp salt

Well ahead, make the marinade by mixing all the ingredients in a glass bowl. Divide this into two portions. Put the large whole prawns into one, mix so that all are well coated and leave in a cool place for up to 1 hour.

Put the other prawns into a blender with the cornflour mixture and egg white and blend to make a smooth prawn paste. Transfer to the second portion of marinade and mix well by hand. Leave in a cool place for up to 1 hour.

When ready to grill and serve, preheat a grill or a ridged griddle pan. Divide the prawn paste into 24 portions. Combine the sesame seeds and rice flour or plain flour on a flat plate and spread them out. Form each portion of prawn paste into a ball and roll it on the flour and sesame seed mixture to coat it all over. On each of the 8 satay sticks, push 4 whole prawns, alternating with prawn balls, so that you have 4 prawns and 3 balls on each skewer.

Brush these satays with a mixture of lemon juice and oil, and grill them for 3–4 minutes, turning them once or twice. Serve hot.

Note: if you make these satays with chicken, duck or pork, the grilling time will be much longer. Allow at least 15 minutes, turning them often.

fish satays

Fish is the real staple food of Southeast Asia. Seafood, river fish and shrimps, fish from lakes and fish reared in domestic ponds – there are fish everywhere, and the ways of cooking them are limitless. This satay is made from fish fillets, which nowadays, especially in the West, are all cleaned and prepared ready to cook. In many Asian markets I have watched fish, large and small, jumping or thrashing about in buckets or on trays of iced water while they wait their turn to be killed, cleaned, gutted and scaled by a group of cheerfully gossiping ladies. Then a large bamboo frame holds the fish as they are barbecued over a bonfire or an open barbecue pit. The eating of them will be just as informal, by hand of course, with gleaming white rice and assorted hot dips and sauces.

makes 8 skewers

**2 medium-sized mackerel, boned and filleted and cut into 8 long pieces, the heads removed, or 8 nice fillets of grouper or snapper
1 tbsp lime juice
½ tsp salt
½ tsp cayenne or white pepper
8 long lemon grass stalks (optional)
Red Pepper and Tomato Sauce (page 163), to serve (optional)**

Rub the fish fillets with lime juice and salt and pepper. Leave them in a cool place for about an hour before grilling them.

Put the fillets on metal skewers or lemon grass stems, starting near one end of the fillet and folding it, first one way, then the other, as you pierce it with the skewer.

Grill or barbecue the satays for about 2 minutes on one side. Turn them over and cook the other side for a little less than 2 minutes.

Serve the satays hot with Red Pepper and Tomato Sauce or any of the piquant sauces on pages 158–9. My choice of accompaniment would be one of the potato croquettes on page 44, as well as some green salad.

minced duck satays

This is one of my favourite satays. Why? I feel good when I am mincing – or chopping with a cleaver – the lovely meat of a pair of duck breasts. Naturally I discard the skin – I don't want the fat, and I don't want that rubbery texture. If you ask me about the new wave marinade for this satay, I shall say simply – salt, crushed garlic and chopped ginger! Then you will get the real taste of the duck, especially if you are lucky enough to live in an area where you can buy Trelough ducks from Herefordshire. If this is not 'new wave' enough for you, see the serving suggestions below.

makes 6-8 skewers

2 pairs of duck breasts (preferably
Trelough, see above), skin removed
1½ tsp fine sea salt
4 garlic cloves, crushed
1 tsp finely chopped ginger
1 tsp grated palm sugar (page 158)
1 tbsp lemon juice
6–8 lemon grass stalks (optional)

to serve (optional)
several kinds of lettuce leaves, lollo
rosso, Cos lettuce, Iceberg, maybe a
few handfuls of pea shoots
(page 22)
Piquant Thai Dressing (page 158)
Peanut Sauce (page 159)
Fresh Tomato Sambal (page 162)

Well ahead, chop the duck breasts into small cubes. Put these in a mincer, or chop them finely with a cleaver or large knife. Knead in the other ingredients until all are well mixed. Chill for at least 2 hours.

When you are ready to grill the satays, divide the duck meat into 8 portions, or more if you prefer your satays smaller. Roll a portion between the palms of your hands, flatten it a little, place a wooden skewer or a lemon grass stalk across it, and mould the meat around the skewer to make a sausage shape. Repeat until all the minced duck portions are skewered.

The best way to grill the satays is on a hot ridged griddle pan, for 6–8 minutes or until nicely browned, turning them over carefully several times.

To serve, I suggest you gather several kinds of lettuce leaves, lollo rosso, Cos lettuce, Iceberg, maybe a few handfuls of pea shoots. Also choose two or three of your favourite sauces from pages 158–63. Lay one lettuce leaf on a plate, then spread on it, say, a teaspoonful of Piquant Thai Dressing. Lay another lettuce leaf on top of the first, and spread the same amount of Peanut Sauce, then another leaf, spread with Fresh Tomato Sambal. Top this with a few more pea shoots and one of the satays – pull the skewer out and discard it. Roll up your lettuce leaves, and take a bite. You must, of course, eat these lettuce-leaf satay rolls by hand – they are fun to eat, and delicious too.

assorted root vegetable satays *Making satays*
and barbecuing them out of doors is such fun that I felt I had to create some satays for vegetarian friends. I find root vegetables easy to prepare, and they go well with Peanut Sauce (page 159), Soy Sauce with Chillies or Coconut Sambal. Here I've also added chunks of slightly unripe plantain, which is not a root vegetable, of course, but is delicious, especially with coconut.

makes 8 skewers or more

1 or 2 sweet potatoes
1 white radish (mooli)
2–3 carrots
2–3 turnips
2 slightly unripe plantains
2 tbsp Soy Sauce with Chillies (page 159)
4 tbsp Fresh Tomato Sambal (page 162)

Preheat the oven to 190°C / 375°F / Gas 5. Peel the vegetables and cut them up into fairly large cubes (about 2.5 cm / 1 inch on a side). Put them into a large zip-lock bag with the sauce and the sambal. Zip the bag shut and roll it, with its contents, to and fro a few times on a flat surface so that the sauce and sambal cover and cling to the vegetable cubes.

Transfer the vegetables to a baking tray, cover the tray with foil and bake in the oven for 25–30 minutes until tender but not too well coloured. Leave them to cool.

When cool enough to handle, spear them on long metal or bamboo skewers. Each skewer should have its fair share of all the vegetables. Up to this point everything can be prepared well in advance, including of course your chosen sauces and sambals.

When you are ready to eat, grill or barbecue the skewers for about 3–4 minutes, turning them often. Serve hot, as suggested above.

grilled stuffed fresh sardines

The best grilled stuffed fish I've ever eaten was in West Java, where they have delicious milkfish that they call bandeng. The Laotians have excellent barbecued flat fish that reminded me very much of Indonesian and Malaysian styles of cooking. The important thing is that the fish must be fresh, and in England I can only get milkfish that's been frozen. So I use fresh sardines. They're not the same as milkfish, but I am very fond of them and they are easily obtained in supermarkets, with their heads removed and all well gutted and cleaned. The stuffing is vegetables and rice; and if you serve these as a main course, rice will make an ideal accompaniment. Alternatively, eat them with chips and a green salad. The stuffing can be cooked in advance and stored in the fridge for up to 48 hours.

for 4 as a main course

16 fresh sardines, without heads, gutted
salt and pepper
2 tsp lemon juice
about 3 tbsp rice flour or plain flour
vegetable oil, for brushing

for the stuffing
3 tbsp vegetable oil
3 shallots, thinly sliced
2 garlic cloves, crushed
2 tsp finely chopped ginger
1 red chilli, deseeded and finely chopped
1 tsp ground coriander
6–8 fresh shiitake mushrooms, thinly sliced
115 g / 4 oz young spinach leaves, roughly shredded
1 green apple, peeled, cored and cubed
60 g / 2 oz cooked rice
2 eggs, separated

Well ahead, open each sardine and press it flat gently, skin side down. Carefully lift out the backbone, sliding your finger under it from the head to the tail and then snapping it off. Discard the bone. Put the fish in a glass bowl, sprinkle with salt and pepper and lemon juice, and turn them so that the seasoning is well spread. Set aside in a cool place for up to 1 hour.

The stuffing has to be cooked before it goes into the fish, so this can be done now or it can be done well ahead. Heat the oil in a wok or shallow saucepan. Stir-fry the shallots, garlic, ginger and chilli for 2 minutes. Add the ground coriander, mushrooms, spinach and apple, and continue stir-frying for a minute or so. Cover the pan for 2 minutes, then uncover and add the rice, mixing everything well and seasoning with salt and pepper. Leave to get cold.

When cold, beat in the egg yolks. Fill each fish with a portion of the stuffing, closing it up as tightly as possible. Alternatively, roll them around the stuffing.

The easiest way to grill the sardines is in a well-oiled ridged griddle pan. Before grilling, dip each fish into the lightly beaten egg whites and roll in flour. Shake off excess flour and brush the fish lightly with oil. Then grill for 3 minutes each side, turning once. Alternatively, deep-fry, arranging them in a deep-fryer basket in one layer, for about 3 minutes. Serve immediately.

grilled boned and stuffed trout

for 4

2 rainbow trout, filleted and with the skin
2 white-fleshed trout, filleted and with the skin
4 tsp lemon juice or lime juice
½ tsp fine sea salt
1 tbsp groundnut or olive oil
2 tbsp chopped mint or coriander leaves
2 tomatoes, skinned and chopped
8 tbsp Coconut Sambal (page 160)

Rub the trout fillets all over with the lemon or lime juice, salt and oil. Arrange the 4 fillets of rainbow trout side by side on a flat surface, skin side down.

Mix the mint or coriander and tomatoes into the sambal, then spread 2 tablespoons of this on each trout fillet. Put the other trout fillets on top.

Wrap each of these fish 'sandwiches' in a square of softened banana leaf (see page 95), or place them side by side in a square wire holder.

Grill the fish, preferably on a barbecue, for 3–4 minutes on each side, turning them only once. Before serving, remove the skin. Serve hot, with a salad.

① ②

the basics of grilling and barbecuing

In hot climates, even in cities, everyone cooks out of doors some of the time and anyone with a good-sized backyard treats it as an extension of the kitchen. My grandmother did most of her cooking in the open, with earthenware pots simmering over wood-fired stoves called *tungku*, which were really just carefully arranged piles of bricks.

In middle-class city households today, in Jakarta, Kuala Lumpur, Singapore or Bangkok, you will find the fancy modern barbecues that are familiar in the West, as well as neat Japanese-style hibachi, and home-made installations that are, indeed, little more than piles of bricks.

Very ancient methods of cooking are still in use and still work well, as long as the cook knows his or her job – spit-roasting, for instance, when a whole goat or suckling pig is to be prepared for a big party; or segments of large green bamboo are used as cooking-pots, filled with minced pork, or chicken or fish in strongly spiced paste, or sticky rice in coconut milk; the bamboo containers are arranged in a line or a circle and the fire built around them.

If barbecuing duck, as here, it would first be marinated in one of the standard local spice mixes. You could use a Balinese mix of finely chopped shallots, garlic and galangal with chilli powder and ground roast coriander and cumin seeds, or a new wave marinade of fine sea salt, crushed garlic cloves, finely chopped ginger and lemon juice.

1 and **2** For a whole duck (with or without its bones): rub the marinade all over and inside the duck, then leave overnight in the fridge. Next day, wrap the duck and the marinade in a large piece of foil. Preheat the oven to 180°C/350°F/Gas 4 and cook the duck for 2 hours, turning down the heat after the first hour to 120°C/250°F/Gas ½. This can be done on the day before you barbecue it, which you can do on any barbecue or charcoal stove. Take off the foil before barbecuing the duck for 30–40 minutes, turning it over several times.

3 For duck breasts, each sliced into 6 or 7 thin slices: marinate the slices overnight in the spice mixture in the fridge. Put each slice on to a bamboo skewer and grill over charcoal for 8–10 minutes, turning the slices several times.

4 For minced duck satay (see page 70): put the skinned duck meat through the mincer, or chop by hand with a large knife or cleaver. Marinate overnight in the fridge. When you are ready to grill, divide the marinated meat into 4–6 portions. Roll each portion into a ball, then push a stem of lemon grass about 20 cm / 8 inches long through it. Re-form the meat into an oval or sausage shape (the marinade will help hold everything together) and grill, on charcoal or under an electric grill, for 8–10 minutes, turning carefully several times.

Jereme Leung's grilled lamb cutlets *I've chosen*

this because of the unusual sauce that accompanies it – what Jereme calls 'an Oriental preserved vegetable sauce'. This dish is a very good example of reciprocal fusion. He served it at Jiang-Nan Chun, the best Chinese restaurant in Singapore, with some excellent mashed potatoes richly laced with herbs. I am equally fond of these cutlets (you can use chops if you prefer) with savoury black rice and mashed sweet potatoes. The black rice will taste excellent with the lamb, and goes perfectly with either kind of mashed potato, contrasting and harmonizing not only in flavour but, rather dramatically, in appearance. The preserved vegetables are to be found in most Asian stores, but if you can't find them cornichons, the little French gherkins, are almost as good.

for 4 as a main course

16 lamb cutlets or 12 large lamb chops
900 g / 2 lb Desirée potatoes or
sweet potatoes, or 225–350 g / 8–12 oz
black glutinous rice (or both)
4 tbsp milk or 115 g / 4 oz double
cream, whipped
60 g / 2 oz butter
1 tbsp finely chopped parsley
1 tbsp freshly chopped thyme
1 tbsp chopped chives
salt and pepper
groundnut or sunflower oil, for frying
chives stalks, to garnish

for the marinade

1 tbsp chopped flat-leaf parsley
1 tbsp chopped chives
1 tbsp chopped mint
1 tsp freshly ground black pepper
2–4 garlic cloves, crushed
½–1 tsp salt
2 tbsp olive oil

for the sauce

225 g / 8 oz canned salted mustard
plant (hum choy) and 225 g / 8 oz
canned preserved mustard plant
(mei choy), or 450 g /
1 lb cornichons
about 600 ml / 1 pt chicken stock
1 tsp sugar
groundnut or sunflower oil, for frying
6 garlic cloves
about 1 tsp oyster sauce
freshly ground black pepper
1 tsp potato starch in 1 tbsp cold water

Well ahead, make the lamb marinade by mixing all the ingredients thoroughly in a bowl. Rub this all over the cutlets or chops and leave to marinate for at least 2 hours or overnight in the fridge.

Make the sauce in advance (the quantities given make quite a large amount, use any left over as a sharp dipping sauce for spring rolls, say): take the salted and preserved vegetables or gherkins out of their cans or jars and rinse them well under cold running water. Then chop them very finely, blanch them in boiling water for 2 minutes, and refresh them under cold running water. Drain in a colander. Put these vegetables in a pan, add the stock and sugar, and bring to the boil. Turn down the heat and let the liquid bubble just a little for 30 minutes. In a wok with a little oil, fry the garlic cloves whole until golden brown. Then chop them finely and add them to the simmering stock. To finish, add the oyster sauce, add pepper to taste and the potato starch mixture. Stir the sauce and keep aside, ready to be reheated shortly before serving.

Now make the mashed potatoes with herbs. If you are using ordinary potatoes, peel them, cut them in halves or quarters and cook in lightly salted boiling water until tender, 18–20 minutes. If using sweet potatoes, peel them, cut into chunks and steam them until tender, 15–18 minutes. Mash the potatoes thoroughly in a large bowl; a potato ricer is the ideal tool for this, but a fork will do. Bring the milk or cream nearly to the boil and add it and the butter and herbs to the potatoes, mashing them all in, and adding salt and pepper if necessary. If you are using black glutinous rice, cook it as described on page 181.

Just before serving, grill the cutlets or chops on a ridged pan or under a grill, or pan-fry them with a little olive oil in a non-stick frying pan. Give them 5 minutes on each side, turning them only once, if you want them medium-rare; if you like them truly rare, 3 minutes on each side is enough.

To serve, put a portion of mashed potatoes on each of 4 warmed dinner plates and arrange the lamb on top. Pour about 2 tablespoonfuls of the reheated sauce over the lamb and garnish with chives.

grilled quails Menado style

These can be grilled very quickly just before serving. They are also ideal for barbecuing in large quantities for summer entertaining, or for taking on a picnic and grilling on a disposable charcoal barbecue. In North Sulawesi, where it originated (Menado is a town in the region), the spice mixture is called rica-rica, *from* mrica, *the Indonesian word for pepper (the letter* c *in Indonesian and Malaysian is pronounced like 'ch' in 'church'.) There, however, they use chicken instead of quail.*

Using the lemon grass stalks as skewers undoubtedly adds even more to the delicious flavour of the birds. **Lemon grass** *(Cymbopogon citratus, see page 133) has become such a well-worn badge of Thai cooking that it is in some danger of being considered a cliché - but it's far too valuable for that. It is a kind of grass, the leaves of which contain aromatic, rather sour-tasting oils. At one time it was grown in Europe as an alternative to tea, for people who found tea indigestible. Later, the oils were used in making perfumes. It is usually sold in small bundles of 4-6 stalks, with the roots cut off and the leaves (or blades of grass) trimmed short. This leaves a fairly thick stem, broadening to a small bulb at the end. The outer leaves, or layers, are dry and faded by this time, but the inner layers are still a rich green colour and quite tender.*

If you are putting in a piece or pieces of lemon grass to flavour a dish, cut off and discard the root end. Chop the stem into two lengths of about 7–10 cm (3–4 in) and throw them in; they are to be removed before the dish is served. If the lemon grass is to be eaten, in a soup or salad, then pull off the dry outer layers and chop the inner part of the stem into thin rounds.

for 4

8 whole quails, cleaned and ready to cook
8 long lemon grass stalks (optional)

for the paste

6–8 shallots or 2 medium onions, chopped
4 garlic cloves, chopped
2–4 large red chillies, deseeded and chopped
1 red pepper, deseeded and chopped
2 tsp chopped ginger
1 tsp crumbled shrimp paste (page 122)
2 tbsp groundnut oil
6–8 red tomatoes, skinned, deseeded and chopped
salt and freshly ground pepper

Put all the ingredients for the paste, except the tomatoes, salt and pepper, into a blender with 2 tablespoons of cold water and blend until smooth. Put the paste in a pan, bring to the boil and simmer for 4 minutes, stirring once or twice. Add the tomatoes and 1 teaspoon of salt and continue cooking the paste for a minute or two more. Adjust the seasoning, adding salt and pepper as required. Remove the pan from the heat and leave it to cool to room temperature.

Preheat the oven to 180°C / 350°F / Gas 4. When the paste is cool, rub it all over the quails. If you like, you can thread each bird with a lemon grass stalk to add flavour and help make the finished effect even more attractive. Put the quail side by side on a large piece of foil, fold the foil over the top to make a loose parcel and the fold the edges to seal it well.

Put the parcel in the oven and bake for about 10 minutes. Preheat a grill or barbecue.

Remove the foil and brush any juices over the birds. Grill or barbecue the quail for 3–4 minutes, turning them over once in this time so that they are well browned all over.

Serve hot with rice, potatoes, noodles or simply with a salad of your choice.

grilled marinated chicken, Khmer style

This is another excellent recipe I received from the chefs at the Grand Hotel d'Angkor. I was so impressed by the flavour of these simple grilled chicken thighs that I have cooked this dish again and again, and it is delicious every time. I wonder if the secret is in the use of fresh turmeric root rather than ground dried (see page 109). The practicalities of new wave cooking here allow the use of commercial curry powder and ground star anise.

for 4 as a main course dish

8 good-sized boned chicken thighs, without skin

for the marinade

2 tsp finely chopped lemon grass, soft inner part only

4 cm / 1½ in piece of fresh turmeric root, peeled and chopped

4 cm / 1½ in piece of fresh galangal (page 109), chopped

2–4 kaffir lime leaves or lemon leaves, chopped

10 garlic cloves, chopped

5 shallots, chopped

1 tbsp roasted peanuts (optional)

2 tsp curry powder (hot or mild)

1 tsp star anise powder

2 tbsp fish sauce (nam pla)

1 tsp sugar

2 tbsp vegetable oil

salt and pepper

to finish or serve (optional)

lots of lemon juice

a little sugar

The day before: make the marinade by blending all the ingredients until you have a reasonably smooth paste. Rub all the chicken thighs with the marinade and refrigerate for 24 hours.

Next day, preheat the oven to 160ºC / 325ºF / Gas 3 and a hot grill. Grill the chicken for a few minutes, turning the pieces several times until they are nicely browned all over.

Put the grilled chicken on a rack in the preheated oven and cook for 40–45 minutes, until well browned

Serve hot. You can moisten these chicken thighs as you serve them either with any leftover marinade or by squeezing lots of lemon juice over them. Alternatively, mix lemon juice with a little sugar and ground pepper, and brush it on the chicken during the last 5 minutes of cooking.

grilled and stuffed Portobello mushrooms

These large open-capped mushrooms are ideal for filling with all sorts of delicious and colourful food. Make sure that the mushrooms and the fillings are all pre-cooked to the point where the final grilling is just a matter of re-heating them and giving them that freshly grilled look.

for 4 people as a starter

4 Portobello mushrooms, stalks removed
2 tsp olive oil
salt and pepper

for the filling

1 large red pepper, deseeded
2 carrots, peeled
2 cm / ¾ in piece of ginger, peeled
2 tbsp olive or sunflower oil
1 large red onion, thinly sliced
1 tbsp light soy sauce
½ tsp salt
½ tsp cayenne or black pepper
115 g / 4 oz mangetout peas, cut at
an angle into tiny sticks
2 large plum tomatoes or vine tomatoes,
skinned, deseeded, and quartered,
then each quarter sliced into three

The mushrooms first need to be baked in an oven preheated to 180°C / 350°F / Gas 4. Before putting them in the oven, brush them all over with a little oil, arrange them gill side up on a baking tray and season well. Bake for 8–10 minutes, remove and leave them to get cold before you arrange the filling on top of them.

To make the filling: cut the pepper and carrots into small sticks and the ginger into thin slices and then into tiny sticks. Blanch the carrots briefly in a pan of boiling salted water, refresh in cold water and drain well. Heat the oil in a wok or shallow pan. When it is hot, add the onion and ginger. Stir, then let them simmer for 2–3 minutes. Add the red pepper and blanched carrots, and stir-fry this mixture for 2 minutes. Add the soy sauce, salt and pepper. Cover the pan and leave it undisturbed for 2 minutes. Uncover, and add the mangetout and the tomato wedges. Stir once, turn off the heat, and cover the pan.

Leave for 2 minutes, then divide the filling equally among the mushrooms, arranged gill side up. Grill for 2 minutes and serve straight away, accompanied by a well-dressed green salad.

grilled stuffed aubergines
All over Southeast Asia, stuffing vegetables with meat, fish or other vegetables usually has two purposes: one is to make the dish go further; the other is to show off skill in cooking. Daughters who have learned to stuff vegetables or fish are considered ready to impress potential in-laws with their talent.

for 4 as a starter or 2 as a vegetarian main course

2 large purple aubergines
1 tbsp chopped creamed coconut
(page 179)
2 tbsp hot water
1 egg
½ tsp salt
vegetable oil, for frying

for the stuffing

2 tbsp sunflower oil
4 shallots or 1 large red onion, thinly sliced
2 tsp finely chopped ginger
2 garlic cloves, finely chopped
6 fresh shiitake mushrooms, thinly sliced
2 tbsp chopped creamed coconut
4 tbsp finely chopped flat-leaf parsley
4 anchovy fillets, chopped (optional)
salt and pepper
2 plum tomatoes, skinned and thinly sliced

Cut the middle part of each aubergine into 4 thick rounds and cube the rest small. Dissolve coconut in the hot water, beat the egg into this and add salt. Coat the aubergine slices in the mix and leave in a cool place for 10 minutes.

Meanwhile, cook the stuffing: heat the oil in a wok or frying pan, add the shallots or onion, ginger and garlic, and stir for 2–3 minutes, until the shallots or onion start to colour a little. Add the mushrooms and cubed aubergine. Continue stirring for a minute or so, then add the chopped creamed coconut and parsley, and the anchovies if using them. Cover for 2 minutes. Uncover, taste, and add salt and pepper as required. Take off the heat and set aside.

When ready to serve, heat some oil in a non-stick frying pan and cook 4 aubergine slices for 3 minutes on each side. Transfer to a plate lined with kitchen paper and repeat with the other 4 slices.

Lay 4 aubergine slices on a flat surface and arrange half the slices of tomato on them. Spread the filling on each, arrange the remaining tomato on top and finally place another slice of aubergine on top to make 4 'sandwiches'. Press down lightly on each to make them firmer and all the same height.

The final cooking can be done by grilling, or in a ridged griddle pan or on a barbecue. Cook for 3–5 minutes, on one side only. Serve hot, as a starter with some salad leaves, or as a main course with rice or new potatoes.

steamed & boiled dishes

Steam cuisine has been quite a trend in the past ten years, for several reasons. It is easy to believe that this must be a healthy way to cook, because it doesn't need oil or any kind of fat. Boiling, by contrast, may seem a little insipid, yet if the liquid contains spices then their flavours will be absorbed by the meat or vegetables that are being boiled. In my Southeast Asian cooking, steaming often means wrapping the meat, vegetables or fish in a small packet made of banana leaf, and steaming them in some sort of container, which may be anything from a sophisticated steam oven in the kitchen of a four-star hotel to a bamboo steaming-basket inside a wok or a saucepan.

steamed or baked salmon and asparagus with piquant dressing

This can be steamed or baked in a casserole dish, or wrapped in baking parchment or banana leaves. As a variation, you can use halibut or tuna steaks. The dressing originated in Thailand, where it is used with vegetables and fruit or noodle salads.

for 4

16 new-season's asparagus stalks
4 salmon fillets, each weighing about
115–150 g / 4–5 oz
1 banana leaf (optional)
2 tbsp fine brown sugar
4 soft-poached eggs (optional)

for the dressing

2 tbsp fish sauce (nam pla)
2 tbsp fresh lime juice
2–4 bird's-eye chillies, deseeded
and finely chopped
2 shallots, thinly sliced
2 tbsp chopped coriander leaves,
plus more for garnish
2 garlic cloves, crushed

If using the oven, preheat it to 180°C / 350°F / Gas 4. Make the dressing by mixing all the ingredients in a glass bowl. Blanch the asparagus in boiling water for 1 minute only, then refresh in cold water. Drain well.

Arrange the salmon fillets side by side in a casserole dish or on a large piece of baking parchment or banana leaf. Sprinkle the sugar on the fish, then pour half the dressing over it. Lay the asparagus on top of the fish and pour over the rest of the dressing. Cover, if using a casserole, or make into a neatly wrapped parcel of banana leaf, sealing the edges by folding them over or securing with toothpicks.

Steam in a large steamer or bake in the oven for 4–6 minutes. Serve hot or cold with new potatoes, rice noodles or pasta. If you are using poached eggs, top each serving with one and garnish with some more coriander.

steamed sea bass with ginger and spring onions, Chinese-style

Rinse the cleaned whole fish under cold running water. If you don't have a large enough steamer or wok, cut the fish in half and put the two halves side by side on the plate. You can also steam in a microwave oven or, of course, in a steam oven. Another alternative is to poach the fish in a fish kettle.

for 4

1 whole sea bass, weighing 450-600 g
/ 1–1¼ lb, gutted and scaled,
gills removed
½ tsp salt
1 tbsp lemon juice
5 cm / 2 in piece of ginger,
peeled and very thinly sliced,
then cut into tiny sticks
4 spring onions, sliced very thinly
at an angle
2 tbsp groundnut oil
2 drops of sesame oil
2 tbsp light soy sauce

Rub the cleaned fish inside and out with the salt and lemon juice. Put the fish on an oval plate and steam it in a large steamer, or a wok with a domed lid, for 8–10 minutes (see also the alternative cooking methods suggested above).

When the fish is cooked, spoon out and discard some of the cooking juices from the plate. Spread the ginger and spring onions on top of the fish. In a small pan, heat the mixed oils until just starting to smoke, and pour them over the ginger and spring onion to cook them slightly. Sprinkle the soy sauce over all and serve at once.

Variation: if you live near a trout farm, a really fresh trout or rainbow trout tastes excellent when cooked this way.

steamed fish in young coconut, Khmer-style

The Khmer name for this is amok. *Though the dish is a traditional one, it has been adopted as a speciality of the Grand Hotel d'Angkor in Siem Reap, which is the ideal base for anyone visiting Angkor Wat and the monuments to the greatness of the ancient Khmer empire. At the Grand, they actually cook and serve this in a young coconut. A wide hole is cut in the top and the coconut water poured off; it makes a delicious drink in the tropical heat. The undisturbed young flesh adds its flavour to the fish.*

I watched this amok *being prepared in the kitchen of the Grand Hotel by a young Cambodian chef and a Balinese sous-chef, supervised by the Singaporean executive chef, Dickson Foo. They were kind enough to give me permission to print the recipe here. As fresh young coconuts don't grow on trees in London, I cook the dish here* en papillote; *you can cook it equally well in large ramekins or in a banana-leaf parcel.*

for 6 as a starter

2–3 fresh trout, each weighing about 350 g / 12 oz, filleted and skinned, then cut into strips about 2 cm / ¾ in wide

4 eggs

1 tbsp grated palm sugar (page 158)

1 tsp salt

175 ml / 6 fl oz thick coconut milk

2 large red chillies, deseeded and cut into julienne strips

3 kaffir lime leaves, cut into fine julienne strips

60 g / 2 oz strands or julienne strips of young coconut flesh (see page 160)

for the paste

175 g / 6 oz lemon grass, soft inner part only, chopped

85 g / 3 oz galangal (page 109), chopped

45 g / 1½ oz turmeric root, chopped, or 1 tsp ground turmeric

45 g / 1½ oz Chinese keys (page 109), chopped

85 g / 3 oz chopped garlic (about 1 large head)

85 g / 3 oz chopped shallots

3-6 dried red chillies, deseeded and chopped

2 tbsp fish sauce (nam pla or nuoc mam, page 164)

4 tbsp thick coconut milk

Make the paste by putting all the ingredients in a blender and blending until smooth. Transfer the paste to a bowl.

In another bowl, whisk the eggs for a minute or two with a hand beater or a fork. Add the sugar, salt and coconut milk, and continue whisking until all are thoroughly mixed. Mix the contents of the two bowls in a single bowl and add the strips of fish. Stir well with a spoon. Taste the sauce, and add a little more salt if needed.

Prepare 6 discs of Bakewell or greaseproof paper about 30 cm / 12 inches in diameter. Divide the fish mixture into 6 portions. Put one portion on the centre of each paper disc. Top with a portion of the chillies, lime leaves and coconut flesh, then fold the disc to make a loose semicircular parcel, sealing it carefully by folding over the edges of the paper.

Steam the parcels in a large steamer or cook them in an oven preheated to 180ºC / 350ºF / Gas 4, setting them over a bain-marie, for 5–6 minutes. In a steamer, the cooking time will be a little shorter, perhaps only 3–4 minutes.

Serve hot as a starter, letting your guests open their parcels for themselves.

steamed savoury fish cake putu ikan

I make no apologies for including another dish created from my Indonesian repertoire. Originally, putu was a sweet snack called 'kueh putu ayu', 'beautiful kueh putu' or 'cupcake' (for a fuller explanation, see the recipe on page 183). Here I have reinvented it as a savoury starter, made with salmon or other fish such as trout or white fish. If you are concerned whether or not the steamed fish cake will separate and come out easily from the ramekins or cups in which it was cooked, use a glass ramekin, bring it to table and serve your putu ikan with a spoon.

makes 12-16 small cups or ramekins

450 g / 1 lb skinned salmon or other fish as above
2 tsp lime juice
2 tsp salt
1 tbsp vegetable oil, plus more for the cups or ramekins
1 garlic clove, crushed
1 tsp ground coriander seeds
4 tbsp coconut cream or single cream (about 6 tbsp if desiccated coconut is used, see below)
a pinch of chilli powder
2 tbsp finely chopped chives
2 tbsp finely chopped parsley or coriander leaves
5 eggs
4 tbsp rice flour
2 tbsp plain flour
1 tsp baking powder
115 g / 4 oz freshly grated coconut or desiccated coconut
½ tsp sugar
a large pinch of ground cumin

Dice the salmon very small, making sure there are no bones left in it. Season with lime juice and a teaspoon of salt. Leave in a cool place until needed.

Heat the oil in a small saucepan. When it is warm, add the garlic and ground coriander. Stir and add 2 tablespoons of the coconut cream or single cream. Then add the chilli powder, remaining salt and the chopped chives and parsley or coriander leaves. Stir all these with a wooden spoon for 2 minutes, then remove from the heat.

Beat the eggs until they turn white. Sift in the flours and baking powder, and mix them well with a fork. Add the rest of the ingredients, including the salmon, and mix again.

Oil the cups or ramekins and heat them in the steamer for 1–2 minutes. When warm, fill them about three-quarters full with the mixture, and steam for 4–6 minutes. Unmould the fish cakes and serve hot or cold.

Variation: use prawns chopped the same way as the salmon or crab meat instead of the fish.

delicately spiced turbot fillets wrapped in Chinese leaves

This is a dish for special people – I like to make it just for two, or at most four. You need all your time and concentration to balance the aromatics and the hot spices, and to get just the right degree of sweetness and sourness in the sauce. Above all, do not overcook the fish. Steaming is a much faster method of cooking than (say) grilling, so you have less margin for error. Wrappings for the steaming of fish vary from country to country, giving subtly different finishes. I think my very untraditional use of orange juice in the marinade helps bring out the flavour of the fish.

makes 2 parcels

2 turbot fillets, each weighing about 175–225 g / 6–8 oz
4 Chinese white cabbage leaves

for the marinade
juice of 2 oranges
juice of 2 lemons
½ tsp salt
1 red chilli, deseeded and finely chopped
½ tsp ground turmeric
1 tsp finely chopped lemon grass
1 tsp caster sugar

for the sauce
2 tbsp vegetable oil or olive oil
2 shallots, finely chopped
2 garlic cloves, finely chopped
1 tsp finely chopped ginger
¼ tsp freshly grated nutmeg
115 ml / 4 fl oz coconut milk or plain yoghurt
salt and pepper
2 tbsp chopped chives
a handful of flat-leaf parsley or coriander leaves

Well ahead, make the marinade by mixing all the ingredients in a glass bowl and marinate the fish in it for at least 2 hours in the refrigerator.

At the end of this time, take the fish out of the marinade and set aside. Reserve the marinade.

Make the sauce: heat the oil in a saucepan and stir-fry the shallots, garlic and ginger until they are all soft (about 3 minutes). Add the reserved marinade, the nutmeg and the coconut milk or yoghurt, and simmer until the sauce is reduced by half. Season to taste with salt and pepper. Set aside.

When ready to serve, blanch the Chinese cabbage leaves in boiling water for 20 seconds and refresh in cold water. Lay the leaves on a flat surface and pat them dry with kitchen paper. Lay 2 leaves side by side, overlapping them a little. On top of them, near one edge, lay a fish fillet coated with as much marinade as you can. Fold the leaves away from you to wrap the fish and place this parcel either on a plate that will fit inside your steamer or on a trivet in a wok. Do the same with the other fillet and steam the parcels for 5–6 minutes.

Just before serving, reheat the sauce in the saucepan and add the chives and the parsley or coriander leaves. Place the fish parcels on a serving dish and pour the sauce over them. Serve hot. Steamed sweet potatoes are particularly good with this dish, together with, of course, a well-dressed salad.

steaming essentials

Steaming has many advantages – the flavour and goodness of the food are preserved, and it's economical in fuel. We steam rice in a rice steamer or double saucepan, and these can also be used to steam little cups or ramekins of savoury food or desserts. A wok makes an excellent steamer, if you have a domed lid; many wok sets include these, and little wire shelves to support the food, though they are usually on rather a small scale. A large-diameter saucepan has the advantage of high sides.

Place in the bottom of it an upturned soup plate or a wire trivet, or anything that will remain reasonably firmly in place and will support the platform – usually another plate or shallow bowl, with the food on it or in it – above the water. This must not bubble over the edge of whatever contains the food, or boil dry. The lid should therefore be as tight-fitting as possible. Some water vapour will still escape, however, and if the steaming goes on for a long time it is obviously wise to check the water level now and then. If necessary, add boiling water.

Steaming in a parcel

This method has all the advantages of steaming but requires no special equipment. It's particularly good for things that won't fit into a regular pan – a fish, for example. You wrap the fish in foil, leaving lots of space for the steam to circulate and sealing the edges carefully so it can't get out.

A steamed whole fish is indeed a classic dish throughout Southeast Asia. Here, I use a small salmon. A large rainbow trout would be equally good, and a sea bass would be delicious. It should weigh up to 2 kg / 4½ lb, not more, when cleaned. If serving it with the skin on, then scale it.

❹ Make some deep slanting cuts on the uppermost side to let both flavourings and heat permeate the flesh. Sprinkle a little salt all over the fish and inside. Put into its cavity a slice of ginger, some garlic cloves and lemon slices. Tie with string around head and body to keep these flavourings in.

❺ Put the fish on a large piece of foil, and turn up the edges to make a kind of shallow dish. Pour 100 ml / 3½ fl oz lightly salted water around the fish.

❻ Bring the edges of the foil together to make the parcel, turning and squeezing them to seal them. Make the parcel much bigger than the fish as the steam must have plenty of space to circulate.

Put in an oven preheated to 180°C/350°F/Gas 4 and cook for 35–40 minutes. Unwrap and transfer the fish to an oval platter.

Cut some spring onions into julienne strips, and cut a few slices of ginger and garlic cloves into even tinier strips. Sprinkle the fish with 1 teaspoon of sugar, then spread the spring onions, garlic, and ginger all over it. Heat 4 tablespoons of groundnut oil in a small pan until very hot.

❼ Pour the hot oil slowly, in a thin stream, all over the fish, moving from head to tail and back again several times. This will cook the spring onion, which will sizzle splendidly. Finally, pour 3 tablespoons of light soy sauce over all; this and the oil combine to make the sauce.

Natural parcels

How did people in Asia steam things in parcels before cooking foil was invented? They used banana leaves, of course, and still do (❶, ❷, ❸ below). Wrapping a big fish in a banana leaf is quite tricky, but small parcels are easy. In West Java, we steam prawns this way with grated fresh coconut, you can use desiccated coconut if you wish.

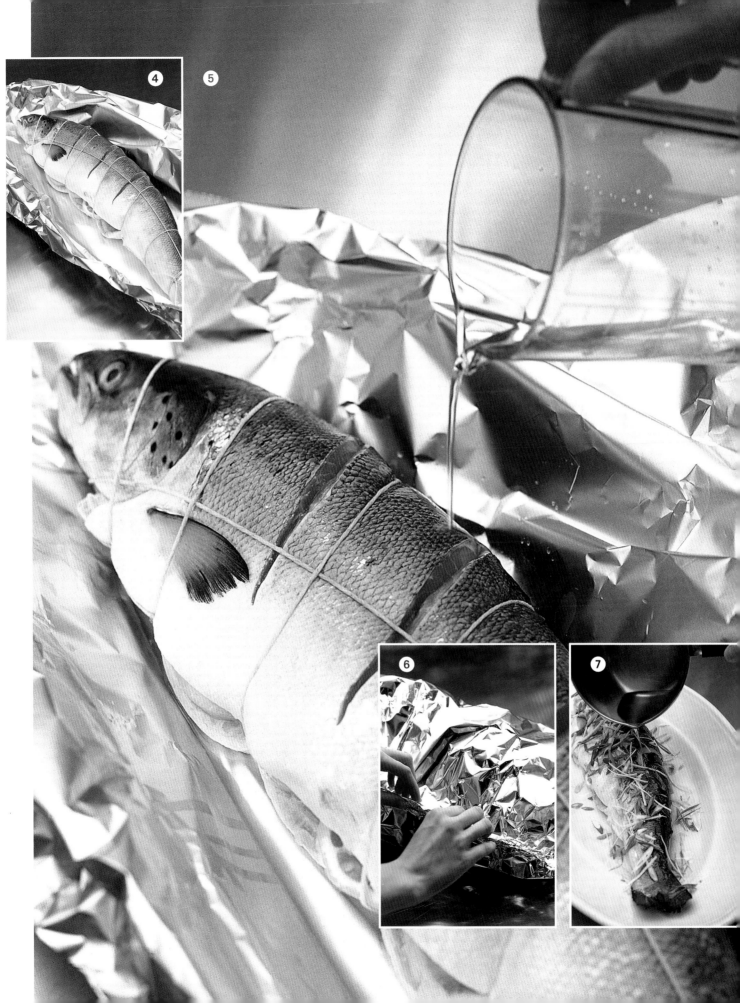

④ ⑤ ⑥ ⑦

steamed chicken with Chinese sausage

This makes a delicious one-pot lunch or supper. If you go to Chinatown for the sausage, you will find several different kinds; the one you want is quite short. A Chinese friend told me to ask for Chinese salami. When I'm shopping elsewhere, I simply buy chorizo as an alternative. This dish would normally be made with chewy dried Chinese black fungus, but I prefer instead to use tasty chestnut mushrooms.

for 6-8

1 free-range chicken, cut through
the bones into about 16 pieces
(see page 174), or 2 chicken legs and
2 chicken breasts, each cut into 3
4–6 dried shiitake mushrooms,
soaked in hot water for at least
20 minutes, then sliced
350–450 g / 12–16 oz Chinese sausage
or chorizo, cut across into slices
about 1 cm / ½ in thick
4–6 fresh chestnut mushrooms, quartered
4 shallots or 1 large onion, chopped
2 tsp chopped ginger
1 tsp sugar
¼ tsp salt
2 tsp cornflour, mixed with
1 tbsp cold water
1–2 tbsp rice wine or dry sherry
¼ tsp cayenne pepper or black pepper
4–5 tbsp light soy sauce
1 tsp sesame oil

Put all the ingredients except half the soy sauce and the sesame oil in a large glass bowl. Mix them well and leave the chicken to marinate for at least 2–3 hours.

When ready to cook, arrange the chicken in a casserole or a dish that will fit your steamer (see page 90). Start with a layer of chicken on the bottom, followed by mushrooms, then sausage, then another layer of chicken, and so on. Pour all the marinade over the contents of the dish and steam for 50–60 minutes.

Finally, pour the remaining soy sauce and the sesame oil over the chicken, and serve at once.

steamed pork fillets stuffed with shiitake, apples, ginger and garlic

This dish preserves authentic Asian flavours, but presents them in a new way. Indeed, there is nothing very new about the combination of all these ingredients in an Asian recipe. Even apples, originally used as a substitute for green mango or some other sour local fruit, are easily available now in tropical Asian countries. They are either imported from China or grown in cool mountain areas such as northern Thailand, where grapes are also grown and wine-making is being tried, with some success. You will see Chinese apples piled up in every market, but I cannot recommend them; they are plump, pink and perfect – and very juicy – but almost totally lacking in flavour. Mountain-grown apples are hard and tart. In Western countries, I would choose Granny Smith's.

for 4 as a main course

4 pork fillets, each weighing about
175 g / 6 oz and 4–5 cm / 2 in thick
2 tsp dark soy sauce
½ tsp cayenne pepper
1 tbsp rice vinegar
a handful of holy basil (page 39),
fried until crisp, to garnish
a handful of raw beansprouts, to garnish
1 tsp thinly sliced red chilli, to garnish

for the stuffing

2 tbsp vegetable oil
5–8 garlic cloves, cut into tiny strips
5 cm / 2 in piece of ginger,
peeled and cut into tiny strips
1 green apple, peeled and cored,
then cut into julienne strips
350 g / 12 oz fresh shiitake mushrooms,
stalks removed, quartered
salt and pepper
1 tsp sugar
8 spring onions, chopped

Make a cut in the centre of the thickness of each pork fillet so that you have a pocket in which to put the stuffing. Mix together the soy sauce, cayenne and vinegar. Rub the fillets with this mixture and leave to marinate.

Cook the stuffing: heat the oil in a wok or saucepan, add the garlic and ginger, and stir for 20 seconds. Then add the apples and mushrooms. Season to taste with salt and pepper and add the sugar. Stir once, then add the spring onions. Continue stir-frying for a further 20 seconds, then leave to cool.

When the stuffing is cool enough to handle, use half of it to stuff the pockets of the pork fillets. Seal the openings with wooden cocktail sticks. Put the stuffed pork fillets on a deep plate that will fit inside your steamer. Steam, covered, for 45 minutes (see pages 90–91 for more on steaming).

Preheat a hot grill. Pour the cooking juices from the steaming plate into the remaining stuffing mix. Arrange the pork fillets on a baking tray and put under the grill for a minute or two so that they get lightly coloured. Heat the stuffing in the saucepan until hot.

To serve, put each fillet on a warmed plate, remove the cocktail sticks and pour the remaining hot stuffing over the pork. Scatter over the garnishes and serve with fried rice, fried noodles or mashed potatoes.

Balinese spiced pork in a banana-leaf

packet *If you feel like being traditional, or if you have a restaurant in Bali and want to attract the tourists, then by all means use banana leaves. If you want to be more practical, cook this in the oven as a large parcel wrapped in foil. The effect is the same: the pork cooks in its own steam inside the wrapping. I explain both methods here. In Bali, people use pigs' blood as one of the ingredients, and as an alternative to this I recommend pigs' liver or black pudding. I love to eat this dish as a starter, with the Avocado, Orange and Beetroot Salad described on page 120.*

for 6-8 as a starter

175–225 g / 6–8 oz loin of pork, cubed,
then chopped finely or minced

115 g / 4 oz pigs' liver, chopped,
or black pudding, skinned
and chopped

115 g / 4 oz fresh shiitake
mushrooms, chopped

10-cm / 4-in length of rhubarb, chopped

3 tbsp chopped flat-leaf parsley

½ tsp salt

1 tsp chopped palm sugar (page 158)
or brown sugar

1 banana leaf (optional, see above)

for the spice mixture

3 shallots, chopped

4 garlic cloves, chopped

2 large green chillies,
deseeded and chopped

2 tsp chopped fresh turmeric

2 tsp chopped ginger root

1 tsp chopped galangal (page 109)

1 tsp chopped Chinese keys
(page 109, optional)

1 tsp grilled and crumbled
shrimp paste (page 122)

1 tsp salt

2 tbsp lemon juice

3 tbsp groundnut oil

First make the spice mixture by blending all the ingredients until smooth. Transfer to a saucepan and simmer, stirring often, for 5–6 minutes. Remove from the heat and leave to cool.

Put all the other ingredients except the banana leaf, if using, in a bowl and, when the spice mixture is cold, mix this in thoroughly, preferably by hand or just by stirring vigorously with a wooden spoon.

If you are using a banana leaf, first soften it by pouring boiling water over it. Cut 6–8 squares each about the size of an A4 sheet of paper. Then put 2 or 3 tablespoonfuls of the mixture in the centre of each square. Fold two opposite edges of the square upwards and fold the two uppermost corners down at an angle of 45°, as if you were making a paper boat. You now have a more or less triangular packet. Secure the closure at the top with a wooden cocktail stick. Repeat until all the mix has been wrapped in this way.

Alternatively, preheat the oven to 180°C / 350°F / Gas 4 and roll the mix on a piece of foil to make a large firm sausage. Unroll the foil and put the unwrapped sausage in the centre of a larger piece of foil. Lift opposite edges of this to make a loose closed packet and crimp the edges of the packet to seal it. There should be plenty of space inside for the steam to circulate and cook the sausage.

The small banana leaf packets can be steamed in a steamer for 40–45 minutes. Cooking time for the sausage in its foil parcel will be about 50 minutes in the oven. Serve hot or warm, as suggested above.

boiled and spiced short rib of beef

Regrettably, 'short rib of beef' is a cut that British butchers no longer supply, so when I am in Britain I use flank instead. It is a perfectly adequate substitute but if you can find short rib use it for this dish. It is equally good hot or cold, accompanied by a cold potato salad or piping-hot fried rice or pasta.

for 4-6 as a main course

675–900 g / 1½–2 lb short rib
or flank of beef, cut into pieces
5–7.5 cm / 2–3 in long and about
2.5–3.5 cm / 1–1½ in thick
1 lemon grass stalk, cut across
into 3 pieces
2.5 cm / 1 in piece of galangal
(page 109), peeled
2 kaffir lime leaves
4 red chillies, deseeded and
cut into 3 pieces
4 green chillies, deseeded and
cut into 3 pieces
6 shallots or 1 large onion, chopped
5 garlic cloves, chopped
1 tsp crumbled shrimp paste (page 122)
4 tbsp tamarind water (page 164)
1 tsp salt

Put the meat in a large pan with 1.1–1.4 litres / 2–2½ pints of cold water. Add the lemon grass, galangal and lime leaves. Bring to the boil, then lower the heat so the water is just bubbling a little. Cook at this rate for 50 minutes, skimming often.

By now the water will have reduced considerably. Add the rest of the ingredients and continue to simmer gently for another 20–25 minutes. The broth will now be quite thick. Taste, and add more salt if necessary. Continue cooking for 5–10 minutes longer. Serve straight away, or leave to get cold and serve as described above.

Variation: if you are cooking this well in advance and want to serve it hot, just heat the meat by grilling or barbecuing. Heat the thick sauce in a saucepan, then brush the sauce on the meat while it is on the grill or barbecue. If you want more sauce, Peanut Sauce (page 159) is an excellent choice.

mixed spiced vegetables wrapped in banana leaves

Every Southeast Asian country – indeed, almost every region – has its own way of cooking mixed vegetables or fish or shellfish in a banana-leaf parcel. This is certainly true of the Central Javanese city of Yogyakarta, where I was a student. A favourite street food was fresh rice-straw mushrooms in banana leaves. When I returned to Yogya in 1987 I met Madhur Jaffrey, who was filming one of her TV series. We went together to taste these delicious mushroom parcels on a street corner near my old university, and the recipe duly found its way into her book. Here is a variation on it, using paria *(bitter gourd), chillies, beansprouts and plenty of mint or holy basil.*

Bitter gourd *or bitter cucumber (*Momordica charantia)*, looks rather like a short cucumber with a knobbly skin. As you might expect, the fruit is bitter in taste and, surprisingly, becomes rapidly more bitter as it ripens, so most people prefer to buy young ones. Older specimens need to be parboiled and then soaked in salt water to remove some of the bitterness.*

makes 6-8 little packets, to be served with a main course

1 medium-sized bitter gourd (not more than 400 g / 14 oz)

salt

115 g / 4 oz beansprouts, roots discarded

1 large red pepper, preferably the large, long Sweet Romano, deseeded and cut into rounds or julienne strips

a handful of mint or holy basil leaves

1 banana leaf

for the spice paste

2 shallots, chopped

2 garlic cloves, chopped

1 tsp chopped ginger

2 candlenuts or macadamia nuts, chopped

1 tsp ground coriander

2 tbsp chopped spring onions

1–3 large chillies, deseeded and chopped

¼ tsp ground turmeric

2 kaffir lime leaves, shredded

115 ml / 4 fl oz coconut milk

Cut the bitter gourd in half lengthwise and spoon out the seeds. Rinse the halves well, slice them thinly into half-moon shapes and put these into a colander. Sprinkle them with 1 tablespoonful of salt, stir well to mix in the salt, then leave for 30 minutes while the bitter juices of the gourd are drawn out by the salt.

At the end of this time, rinse well under cold running water and leave to drain again for 30 minutes, or pat dry with kitchen paper.

Make the spice paste by putting all the ingredients except the coconut milk in a blender with salt to taste and blending until smooth. Put the paste into a saucepan and bring it to the boil, then simmer, stirring often, for 7–8 minutes. Add the coconut milk and continue cooking until reduced by half and nicely thick.

Add the bitter gourd slices and cook for 3 minutes on a low heat. Add the beansprouts and pepper, stir for 2 minutes, then add the mint or basil and adjust the seasoning.

Now prepare the banana leaf, which has been softened by pouring boiling water over it. Cut a piece about 20 cm / 8 in square. Lay this on a flat surface and put 2 tablespoonfuls of the cooked vegetables on the centre of the square. Then wrap the vegetables and complete the parcel as described on page 95.

When you have wrapped all the vegetables, put the packets in a steamer and steam for 5 minutes. Serve them straight away, unopened, as the vegetable side dish to accompany a main course. Let everyone open their own banana-leaf parcel so that they enjoy the aromas that rise from it.

boiled and spiced tofu

This is another good way to make tofu more interesting. Readers in Central Java will not find anything very novel here, as this dish has been cooked in every household and has appeared on every small restaurant menu for generations, perhaps centuries. However, it will probably be new to most people outside Indonesia, even to other Southeast Asians, as they always seem to follow the Chinese when they cook tofu. This is dedicated to my vegetarian friends in the West.

for 4 as a main course

4 blocks of Chinese-style tofu, each 450 g / 1 lb, cut in half
groundnut oil, for frying

for the spice mix
4 shallots, finely chopped
2 garlic cloves, finely chopped
2 tsp finely chopped ginger
1 tsp finely chopped galangal (page 109)
4 tbsp tamarind water (page 164)
2 tsp grated or chopped palm sugar
1–1½ tsp salt
¼ tsp cayenne pepper
1 tbsp dark soy sauce
2 kaffir lime leaves (optional)

Put the tofu and all the ingredients of the spice mix in a saucepan with 225-350 ml / 8–12 fl oz cold water, or to cover. Bring to the boil and keep boiling until almost all the liquid is gone. Taste and adjust the seasoning. Leave the tofu to cool.

When the tofu is cold, cut the halves in two again. Heat the oil in a non-stick frying pan and fry the tofu pieces in batches of 4 for 3 minutes on each side, turning them once. Drain on kitchen paper.

Serve hot or warm as a main course, accompanied by rice, pasta or potatoes.

steamed tofu sandwich with crabmeat

Tofu is an excellent source of protein for vegetarians, so really strict vegetarians can replace the crabmeat with wild asparagus or Thai baby asparagus. If you do use crabmeat, it must be only the best and the freshest. Failing that, use finely chopped raw prawns.

for 4 as a first course,
or 2 as a light main course

225 g / 8 oz crabmeat, white meat only
white of 1 egg
1 tsp finely chopped ginger
1 garlic clove, finely chopped
a pinch of cayenne pepper
½ tsp sesame oil
salt
450 g / 1 lb tofu
4–6 spring onions, thinly cut at an angle
1 red chilli, deseeded and thinly sliced
2 tbsp dark soy sauce
3 tbsp sunflower oil

In a glass bowl, combine the crabmeat with the egg white, ginger, garlic, cayenne pepper, sesame oil and a pinch of salt.

Cut the tofu into quarters and then each quarter into halves to make 8 thin rectangles. Put 4 of these thin slices of tofu side by side on a plate that will fit inside your steamer. Arrange equal portions of the crabmeat mixture on these slices, then lay the remaining slices on top to make 4 sandwiches.

Put the plate of sandwiches in the steamer, cover and steam for 5 minutes. Remove from the steamer. Spread the spring onions and chilli all over, followed by the soy sauce.

Just before serving, heat the oil in a small pan until it starts to smoke. Pour this hot oil slowly over the spring onions and chillies. Serve straight away as a starter, with some salad, or as a main course dish with pasta, noodles or new potatoes.

curries and long-cooked dishes

'Curry' in the West has become a catch-all term, often applied to vaguely Asian dishes that are not true curries at all. Even in Asia, the word is used rather loosely, but no one doubts that one of its true meanings is 'a stew with sauce'. This is certainly how I interpret curry in these recipes: a stew or a long-cooked dish, with a delicious and harmonious combination of spices that produce a good rich, tasty sauce. There are variations on the curry theme in this book, drawn from different Southeast Asian countries, where cattle and poultry are free-range to the point of becoming lean, muscular and pretty tough. The spices and the long cooking have a practical purpose: to tenderize the meat and penetrate it with flavour. Fish and seafood, by contrast, can be quickly ruined by overcooking, which accounts for my repeated suggestions that this should be avoided.

Burmese chicken curry with limes and tomatoes

This is one of the easiest curries to make. It's also very popular with children, perhaps because, though it is an authentic Burmese curry, it is not made with coconut milk or yoghurt, but with tomatoes. Use fresh tomatoes if you have an abundance during the summer in your garden – they must be very ripe. Otherwise, your curry will be just as good with the best canned chopped plum tomatoes you can get. The real difference between this curry and those of other Southeast Asian countries is that one of the ingredients is an authentic Burmese balachaung (page 160), but the children won't notice, as long as you reduce the amount of chillies.

for 6

2 tbsp groundnut oil
1 tbsp sesame oil
2 onions, finely chopped
2 garlic cloves, finely chopped
1 tsp ground turmeric
1 tbsp ground coriander
2 cinnamon sticks
4 cloves
1 lemon grass stalks, cut into 2 pieces
4 kaffir lime leaves
4 chicken breast fillets and 8 boned chicken thighs, with or without skins
450 g / 1 lb ripe tomatoes, skinned and chopped, or 450 g / 1 lb can plum tomatoes with their liquid
juice of 2–3 limes
3 tbsp Balachaung (see page 160)
½ tsp cayenne pepper (optional)
1 tbsp fish sauce (nam pla)
4 tbsp hot water
a little salt if needed

Preheat the oven to 160ºC / 325ºF / Gas 3. Heat both oils in a large pan and, when hot, stir-fry the onions and garlic, stirring often, for 2–3 minutes. Add the turmeric, ground coriander, cinnamon, cloves, lemon grass, lime leaves and chicken pieces. Stir until the chicken pieces are lightly browned.

Add the rest of the ingredients except the hot water and salt. Cover and simmer for 3 minutes. Add the water and salt, cover again and cook for another 15–20 minutes on a moderate heat.

Transfer the chicken pieces to an ovenproof dish and put them in the oven, leaving the sauce to continue cooking until it has become thick and oily, about 10–15 minutes. Spoon out some of the oil and discard it. Adjust the seasoning, adding salt if needed.

Take the chicken from the oven and pour the curry sauce over it. Serve hot straight away, with plenty of plain boiled rice.

Filipino chicken adobo

Adobong manok *is the Filipino name for this. The sauce should be quite thick, to concentrate the flavour, so the time taken in reducing it is well spent. The sauce is reddish-yellow, and was originally coloured by paprika and annato seeds, but I always replace annato with turmeric (the former is now thought to be potentially toxic while the latter is a potent natural antiseptic and has lots of other beneficial properties.)*

for 4–6

1.1–1.4 kg / 2½–3 lb chicken, cut into serving pieces, the fat and skin discarded

6–8 garlic cloves, finely chopped

115 ml / 4 fl oz white vinegar or rice vinegar

1 or 2 kaffir lime or bay leaves

½–1 tsp coarsely ground black pepper or chopped chillies

1 tsp salt

2 tbsp groundnut oil

½–1 tsp ground turmeric

½–1 tsp paprika

150 ml / ¼ pt very thick coconut milk

2 tbsp fish sauce (nam pla or nuoc mam) or light soy sauce

Put the chicken pieces in a large pan, add the garlic, vinegar, lime or bay leaves, pepper or chillies, salt and 1.1 litres / 2 pints water. Bring to the boil, cover, reduce the heat and simmer for 20 minutes.

With a slotted spoon, transfer the chicken pieces to a colander. Turn the heat up under the pan and boil the stock until reduced by half, about 20–25 minutes.

Heat the oil in another pan and add the turmeric and paprika. Stir and add about 6 tablespoons of the coconut milk. Stir once and put in the chicken pieces. Stir these until every piece is coated in the sauce.

Pour in the reduced stock from the other pan and the rest of the coconut milk. Bring to the boil and let bubble gently, stirring often, for 15–20 minutes.

Add the fish sauce or soy sauce, adjust the seasoning, and serve hot, with plain boiled rice, mashed potatoes or pasta.

duck long-cooked in rich coconut sauce

It's always useful to have a good repertoire of recipes that are quick and easy to prepare. This one is, in fact, for a traditional Sumatran dish in which the duck is left pretty much to itself during cooking, right up to the final few minutes before serving.

for 4

4 duck breasts, each cut in half and the skin discarded

6 shallots, finely chopped

3 garlic cloves, finely chopped

2 tsp finely chopped ginger root

2 tsp finely chopped fresh turmeric

2 tsp finely chopped galangal (page 109)

1 tsp cayenne pepper

1.7 litres / 3 pt thick coconut milk

2 kaffir lime leaves or bay leaves

1 tsp salt, or more to taste

Put all the ingredients in a heavy ovenproof pan and bring to the boil over a medium heat, then leave to bubble gently for 1 hour. By this time the sauce will have reduced considerably.

Preheat the oven to 150°C / 300°F / Gas 2. Turn the heat under the pan to high and cook for about 10 minutes more, stirring from time to time.

Cover and place in the preheated oven for another hour. The dish is now ready. Take it out of the oven and put it on a low heat on the stove and stir until the sauce is nicely amalgamated. Adjust the seasoning and serve with rice or pasta.

pepper-crusted fillet steak with mild

curry sauce
This fillet of beef is coated with a sauce which the executive sous-chef at Le Royal Hotel in Phnom Penh tells me is the authentic dipping sauce for a Khmer dish called Beef Loc-lac. I know this is a delicious dish, because he cooked it for me, but no one has yet been able to tell me what loc-lac means.

The sauce is made from coarsely ground black pepper mixed with lemon juice (or lime juice, if you prefer) and salt. Naturally I wanted to see what new dish I could make of this. So here I use the combination of pepper, lemon juice and salt first as a marinade, then as a crust for the beef before I cook the steaks on a griddle, or under the grill, until just medium-rare. I am including the recipe in the section on curries because the Mild Curry Sauce on page 163 makes the perfect accompaniment. Allow one good-sized steak per person as a main course dish. I suggest you serve this with straw potatoes.

for 4

3 tbsp coarsely ground black pepper

juice of 1 juicy lemon or lime

1–2 tsp coarse sea salt

4 fillet steaks, each weighing
150–180 g / 5–6 oz

2 tbsp soft butter

Mild Curry Sauce (page 163), to serve

Mix the pepper, lemon or lime juice and salt. Set aside half of this mixture and use the rest to marinate the steaks. Rub them well with the marinade, then leave them in a cool place for 1 hour.

When ready to serve, heat a grill or a griddle pan. Rub the soft butter all over the steaks, then coat them with the rest of the pepper mixture. Cook the steaks for about 2 minutes on one side, then turn them over and cook on the other side for 2 more minutes. If you don't want your steaks as rare as this, cook them for a minute or two longer.

To serve, cut the steak into 3 or 4 slices. Pile the accompaniments next to the steak. (As an alternative to crisp straw potatoes, I would suggest vegetable tempura, see pages 21 and 62–3, or the vegetable crisps that you can now buy in packets in good delicatessens.)

Serve the curry sauce hot in small individual bowls so that diners can help themselves and pour it over the beef.

slow-cooked lamb with water spinach

In most parts of Southeast Asia you will see goats rather than sheep. Goat meat needs to be cooked slowly if you want to make it tender and full-flavoured, mingling beautifully with aromatic spices and hot peppers. However, I think most people would rather eat lamb, and here I use lamb shanks on the bone and not too many spices. The sauce has four of those tastes vital to Asian cooking: sweet, sour, hot and salty. If you cannot get water spinach, don't use ordinary spinach as a substitute as it is too soft; use Swiss chard instead.

for 4-6

2 lamb shanks on the bone

2–4 tbsp groundnut oil

2 large onions, chopped

6 garlic cloves, chopped

2 tsp chopped ginger root

1 tsp cayenne pepper

2 tsp ground coriander

1 tsp ground turmeric

4 tbsp tamarind water (page 164)

900 ml / 1½ pt hot water

2 large red chillies, deseeded and thinly sliced at an angle

2 tsp grated palm sugar or soft brown sugar

1 tsp salt

1 lemon grass stalk, cut across into 3

6 cm / 2½ in piece of galangal (page 109), peeled and washed

675–800 g / 1½–1¾ lb water spinach (page 28), trimmed

juice of 1 lime

4 tbsp chopped flat-leaf parsley

4 red plum tomatoes, skinned, deseeded and roughly chopped

Unless the butcher has already done this for you, trim off and discard some of the fat from the lamb.

Heat the oil in a large heavy pan and fry the onions for 4 minutes, stirring often. Add the garlic, ginger, cayenne, coriander and turmeric. Stir for a minute, then add the tamarind water. Stir again and put in the lamb. Move the pieces around so they are coated all over with the spice mixture.

Add the hot water, chillies, sugar, salt, lemon grass and galangal. Bring to the boil, cover the pan, lower the heat and cook slowly for 1 hour. Then add a little more hot water and continue cooking for a further 1 hour, either on the stove or in the oven as below.

If you wish, you can finish cooking in an oven, preheated to 130°C / 275°F / Gas 1. The pan should be tightly covered. If you prefer to continue cooking on top of the stove, keep the pan covered but look at the contents from time to time and add more hot water when required, so that when the lamb is done there will be plenty of sauce in the pan.

About 10–15 minutes before the end of the second hour, add the lime juice, parsley and tomatoes. At the end of the second hour, taste and add more salt, sugar and pepper as needed. Instead of salt, you can, if you prefer, add 1 teaspoon of nam pla fish sauce. If you were cooking in the oven, take the pan out.

About 10 minutes before you are ready to serve, take out the meat and put it on a wooden board. Remove and discard the pieces of galangal and lemon grass from the sauce. Heat the sauce on the stove, add the water spinach and put the shanks back into the pan on top of the water spinach. Cover the pan and simmer for 5 minutes, then serve hot, with rice, pasta or potatoes.

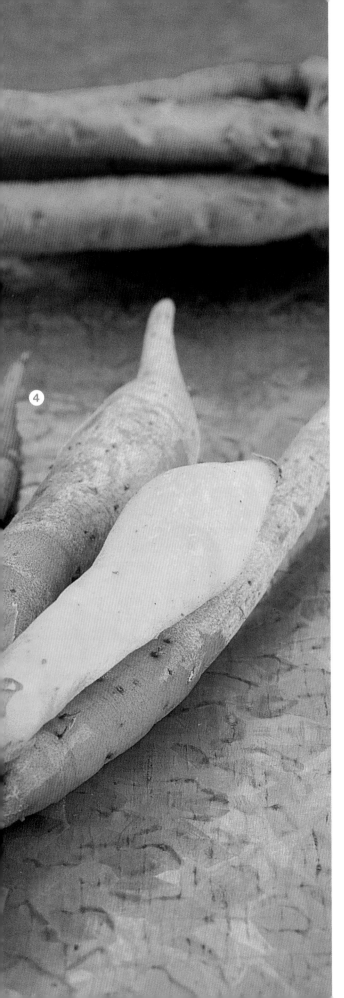

some asian roots

These rhizomes are earthy not only in origin but in colour and flavour. All are valued for their medicinal properties as well as for the subtlety they give to dishes that contain them.

Turmeric (*Curcuma longa*) Fresh turmeric (**1**, top) is better, but if you can't get it, it's quite alright to use ground turmeric (**1**, bottom). Fresh turmeric must, of course, be peeled before use. Remember that turmeric contains a powerful bright-yellow dye that is almost impossible to wash out if it gets on your clothes. I've often wondered if this is why yellow, in Southeast Asia, has long been regarded as a semi-divine colour, to be used only by royalty. On a more practical level, turmeric dyes rice yellow in the same way as saffron, but at a fraction of the cost. (Admittedly, saffron has more flavour.)

Galangal (*Alpinia galangal*) This pinkish-white rhizome **2** can be bought fresh in most Thai food shops in big cities and can be frozen. It is a real Asian flavour and although it has a somewhat gingery aroma, it is less hot than ginger and more sour.

Ginger (*Zingiber officinale*) I am sure it is unnecessary to tell readers of this book always to use fresh ginger **3**. If you prefer the hotness of ginger to that of chillies, then slice your ginger, boil it for 3 minutes and strain the liquid. This 'ginger water' is good to drink as tea, with added sugar or honey if you wish. It is equally good when added to broth for soup, as in the Vietnamese Hot and Sour Soup of Duck on page 28.

Ginger juice is made by grating, say, 60 g/2 oz of peeled ginger root and pressing the juice out of it. Add a teaspoonful or so of tepid water to the gratings and let them steep for a couple of minutes; this makes the juice flow more easily. A garlic press is a good way to apply pressure.

Young ginger (**3**, bottom) is often available in the West in Oriental grocers and supermarkets. The taste is milder and thin slices combine well with any salad. You can make a delicious relish to go with satays or roast or cold meats by marinating sliced young ginger for an hour or so in Piquant Vietnamese Dip (page 158).

Chinese keys (*Boesenbergia pandurata*) Known in Indonesia as *kunci* and as *kra chai* to the Thais, this member of the ginger family is sold in many Thai and other Oriental food shops in the West, usually fresh. A root of it **4** looks like a bunch of thin brown fingers joined to a yellowish corm; its resemblance to a bunch of old-fashioned Chinese keys gives it its familiar name. It is used all over Southeast Asia, as well as in south India and Sri Lanka, for the pleasant aroma it gives to savoury dishes. It is regularly used in Thailand and Cambodia for a wide variety of curry pastes and soups.

long-cooked pork loin chops stuffed with pineapples

For these, the meat needs to be sufficiently thick and wide for a pocket to be cut in one side of it to take the pineapple stuffing. A short wooden skewer is enough to close the opening. This is an excellent dish to make for a large party; it is quite easy to prepare and can be left in the oven for up to 3 hours. You can put it in long before your guests arrive, and know that it will be beautifully cooked just at the right time to be served as the main course.

for 10

5–7 tbsp Rujak Sauce (page 169)

1 pineapple, peeled, cored and cubed

10 thick-cut pork loin chops, each weighing about 150–175 g / 5–6 oz

4 shallots, finely chopped

4 garlic cloves, finely chopped

2 tsp finely chopped ginger

600 ml / 1 pt chicken or vegetable stock (page 174)

salt and pepper

At least 3½ hours before you want to eat, mix the Rujak Sauce with the pineapple cubes in a bowl. Make a deep incision on one side of each pork chop. Stuff the chops with the pineapple mixture. Secure the openings with wooden skewers. Arrange the pork chops in a casserole, packing them tightly together. If there is any stuffing left over, spread it on top of them.

Mix in, as well as you can, the shallots, garlic and ginger. Season the stock with salt and pepper, and pour it over the meat. Cover the casserole and leave the meat to marinate for an hour or so. Preheat the oven to 180°C / 350°F / Gas 4.

Put the covered casserole in the oven and cook for 1 hour. Turn down the oven to 100°C / 210°F / Gas ¼ and let the meat cook for at least another hour more, or up to 3 hours.

About 15 minutes before you are ready to serve, take the casserole out of the oven. Arrange the pork chops side by side on a flameproof plate. Put the plate back in the oven to keep the chops warm, or under the grill to let them brown a little.

Meanwhile, if there is a lot of sauce still in the casserole, put the casserole on the stove over a medium heat to reduce it. However, if the casserole has been in the oven for more than 2 hours, the sauce should be very thick. In this case, add more stock or coconut milk to liquefy the sauce quickly, but don't make it too thin. Adjust the seasoning with salt and pepper if needed. This sauce can be poured over the meat before serving, or can be served separately in a sauceboat.

poached egg sambal goreng
The word 'sambal' occurs in many parts of Southeast Asia, and generally means some kind of chilli sauce or a relish of crushed chillies. A sambal goreng is a stew or curry that contains a sambal and spice mixture cooked with coconut milk. To completely identify the dish, all you then have to give is the name of the principal ingredient: for example, sambal goreng udang *is prawn* sambal. *Beef and chicken* sambals *are popular, and a hard-boiled egg* sambal *is a good old family stand-by. For a softer-textured egg, and a more appetizing presentation, I prefer to poach my eggs. Boiled rice, mashed potatoes or boiled new potatoes with lightly braised spinach or pak choy make very suitable accompaniments.*

for 4

1 recipe quantity Spice Paste from Sambal Goreng Sauce recipe (page 162)
225 ml / 8 fl oz thick coconut milk
salt
8 large eggs (preferably organic free-range)
3 ripe tomatoes, skinned and chopped, and most of the seeds removed

Make the paste as described on page 162. Transfer the paste to a saucepan, bring to the boil and simmer, stirring often, for 6–8 minutes.

Add the coconut milk and bring to the boil again. Lower the heat and simmer for about 10 minutes, stirring from time to time. Adjust the seasoning, adding more salt if necessary. Keep this sauce in a cool place until needed.

When ready to serve, poach the eggs: bring to the boil about 600 ml / 1 pint of water with a few drops of mild vinegar in a frying pan. Break each egg and drop it straight into the boiling water, from a point as close to the surface of the water as possible. Cover the pan tightly, and leave them in the water for 3 minutes, undisturbed. The eggs will then be ready – you will see that the whites have become opaque and the yolks are covered by a thin translucent white layer. With a slotted spoon, lift the eggs out of the water, one at a time, and put them gently into a shallow bowl about a quarter full of cold water. This will stop them cooking. You may have to do this in batches.

Reheat the sauce and, when it is almost boiling, add the chopped tomatoes and continue to simmer for 2 minutes. Scoop the poached eggs from their bowls and put them on a flat surface – a tray or a flat plate. With a small knife, trim off any bits of white that have spread too far, so that you have nicely shaped eggs. Put these into the hot sauce to re-heat them for 1 minute only. Serve hot straight away.

jungle curry of pork spare ribs

This jungle curry has a good strong flavour and, after some experimenting, I find that spare ribs of pork are just the right meat for it. I suggest you choose the American cut for the ribs – that way, there is always plenty of meat on the bones. Chop them into short pieces, 5–8 cm / 2–3 inches long, before cooking; this looks more appetizing than if they were uncut. You don't need to make this curry too chilli-hot. I would rather concentrate on the aubergines – I like at least three different kinds, one of which should be pea aubergines (for more on aubergines, see pages 46–7). That's enough clues now for you to know that this must be based on one of the many curries of Thailand.

for 6–8

1 recipe quantity Jungle Curry Paste (page 168)
1 kg / 2¼ lb pork spare ribs, cut into 5–8 cm / 2–3 in lengths
salt
1.4 litres / 2½ pt hot water
115 g / 4 oz thinly sliced bamboo shoots
225 g / 8 oz pea aubergines
8–10 apple aubergines, cut in halves
8 baby purple aubergines, cut in half lengthwise
fish sauce, to taste
lots of coriander leaves, mint leaves and holy basil leaves, to garnish

Make the paste as described on page 168. Transfer to a large pan, bring to the boil, then simmer, stirring often, for 4–6 minutes.

Meanwhile, put in the spare ribs in another large saucepan, cover them with about 1.7 litres / 3 pints cold water and add 1 teaspoon of salt. Bring to the boil and boil for 5 minutes. Drain the ribs in a colander and discard the water. Put the ribs into the pan with the paste and stir them around so that they are well coated with it. Add the hot water, cover the pan and cook for 45–50 minutes.

Uncover the pan, add the bamboo shoots and pea aubergines, and continue cooking for 2 minutes, then add the other aubergines. Adjust the seasoning to taste by adding fish sauce. If the curry sauce is getting too thick, add a little more hot water. Cook the curry on a medium heat for 10 more minutes.

Add the herbs for just the last minute of cooking before transferring the curry to a large serving bowl. Serve piping hot, with plain boiled jasmine rice.

fried prawns in red curry sauce

If you are travelling in Southeast Asia, this is a prawn dish that you will encounter everywhere, in one form or another. Prawns are plentiful and cheap in those parts, and everyone knows that there are countless variations on curry. Local people buy this, ready-cooked, from street vendors and takeaways (invented in Asia long ago) or they make it at home. There the cook is usually a 'helper' or a member of the family who is accustomed, or expected, to get up early in the morning and prepare all the meals for the day.

The new twist in this recipe is that the prawns, instead of being cooked at breakfast time for half an hour or so and kept in the kitchen until the evening, are fried only for a few minutes at the last moment, to be served piping hot. If you have made your curry paste in advance and stored it in the fridge or freezer, you can have a cooked supper on the table very quickly.

To clean prawns, first remove their heads and shells, but leaving the tails on. With a sharp knife, cut from the head end down the middle of the back, about two-thirds of the way to the tail. Make sure you cut right through the prawn. Then open the prawn like a book, so that it looks like a butterfly. This will reveal the black 'vein' (actually the intestine) near the head end. This should lift out on the point of your knife. Discard.

for 4

2 tbsp plain flour
½ tsp salt
12–16 large raw tiger prawns, shelled, butterflied and deveined as above
6 tbsp Red Curry Paste (page 166)
225 ml / 8 fl oz thick coconut milk
115 ml / 4 fl oz groundnut oil
salt and pepper

Combine the flour and salt, and coat the prawns with this. Set aside.

Put the curry paste and coconut milk in a saucepan and bring them to the boil. When boiling, stir the sauce and reduce the heat. Leave to simmer gently while you deep-fry the prawns.

Heat the oil in a saucepan or wok. Fry the prawns in 2 batches for 3 minutes each batch.

Adjust the seasoning of the sauce and put the fried prawns in it for a few seconds, then serve immediately. Traditionally, in Asia these are eaten with rice, but you can equally well serve them with pasta or mashed potato.

green curry of tofu, courgettes and courgette flowers

With tofu and courgettes, the green curry sauce need only be poured over them during the last minutes of cooking. The curry paste can be made well in advance and frozen in ice-cube trays (see page 166). If you can get them, use the small courgettes with the flowers still unopened and attached to the baby courgettes. If you are not fond of tofu, you could replace it with white fish steaks.

for 4

2 tbsp groundnut oil
450 g / 1 lb Chinese-style tofu, quartered and then quartered again, to give 16 pieces
2 tbsp light soy sauce
8 baby courgettes, with flowers if possible

for the green curry sauce

6 tbsp Green Curry Paste (page 166) or 3 curry paste cubes
6–8 tbsp Greek-style yoghurt
4 tbsp hot (but not boiling) water
2 tsp fish sauce (nam pla) and/or salt to taste

Make the sauce: put the curry paste and 4 tablespoons cold water in a pan. Heat, stirring frequently, until it boils. Transfer the yoghurt to a bowl, add the hot water and whisk until it becomes smooth and runny. Pour this into the pan with the curry paste and continue stirring for a minute or so. Now add 4 more tablespoonfuls of cold water and simmer for 3–4 minutes more. Season with the fish sauce and/or a little more salt if necessary. Remove from heat.

Heat the oil in a large, shallow non-stick saucepan. When hot, add the tofu pieces and leave to fry undisturbed for 2 minutes on one side, then turn them over. Add the soy sauce, followed by the courgettes (and flowers, if any) and 4 tablespoonfuls of the curry sauce (any unused sauce can be frozen in ice-cube trays for future meals). Cover, lower the heat and simmer for 4 minutes.

When ready to serve, pour the curry sauce into the pan with the tofu and courgettes, and cook for a further 3–4 minutes on a low heat. Serve hot with rice, boiled new potatoes or pasta.

green curry of red snapper

This needs no introduction, except for the usual reminder that the fish must not be overcooked. Grey mullet or monkfish will be good alternatives to the snapper. Green curries are usually made with chicken or pork, but the flavour also suits fish very well.

for 4

about 900 g / 2 lb fillets of snapper, grey mullet or monkfish
1–2 tbsp olive oil
2 tbsp rice vinegar
¼ tsp salt
6 tbsp Green Curry Paste (page 166)
8 tbsp plain yoghurt or 175 ml / 6 fl oz coconut milk

to garnish

coriander leaves
a handful of pea shoots
30–60 g / 1–2 oz Crisp-fried Ginger (page 170)

Cut the fish fillets into pieces about 5 cm / 2 inches square and 2 cm / ¾ inch thick. Heat a frying pan, preferably non-stick and add the oil, tilting the pan to spread it across the whole surface. Arrange the fish pieces side by side, close together, add the vinegar and sprinkle the salt all over. Shake the pan a little and cover. Leave the fish to steam on a low heat for about 4 minutes. Turn the fillets over, cover again and cook for 2–3 minutes more. Turn off the heat, uncover and leave the fish to cool.

Heat the curry paste gently in a saucepan and, when hot, add the yoghurt or coconut milk. Keep on a low heat for 6–8 minutes. Adjust the seasoning by adding more salt if necessary.

When ready to eat, add the pieces of fish with the cooking juices to the pan of sauce. Cook for 2 minutes, then add the coriander leaves and pea shoots so they wilt a little, about 30 seconds. Serve, garnished with the crisp ginger, as a light lunch, with the Avocado and Orange Salad (page 120).

sour orange curry of blue cod and cabbage

I first got to know this curry when I ordered it at David Thompson's Sailor's Thai restaurant in Sydney several years ago. David was famous for his cooking at Darley Street Thai, the restaurant he has now sold. He is still a part-owner of Sailor's Thai and the food there is, for me anyway, no less authentic, and at the same time simpler but more exciting. The 'blue cod' is the Australian blue-spotted rock cod. The curry is called 'sour' because of tamarind and 'orange' because of its colour. There are, as you probably know, several different colours of curry: green, red, yellow and orange. The colours of the first three depend simply on the chillies and peppers that are used – but the orange gets its colour from red chillies and turmeric.

for 6

6 cod fillets, each about
150–175 g / 5–6 oz
salt
300 ml / ½ pt fish or chicken stock
(pages 174–5)
4–6 Savoy cabbage leaves,
or Chinese leaves (see page 25),
washed and roughly shredded
1 tbsp tamarind water (page 164)
1 tsp fish sauce (nam pla)
a handful of mint leaves

for the orange curry paste
4–6 large red chillies,
deseeded and chopped
4 shallots, chopped
2 garlic cloves, chopped
1 tsp chopped galangal (page 109)
1 tbsp dried shrimps (page 164),
soaked in hot water for
5 minutes, then chopped
½ tsp salt
¼ tsp sugar
a large pinch of ground turmeric
5 tbsp thick tamarind water (page 164)
2 tbsp groundnut oil

If necessary, skin the fish fillets, then rub them all over with a little salt.

Make the curry paste by putting all the ingredients in a food processor or blender and blending until smooth. Transfer to a saucepan, bring to the boil and cook, stirring continuously for 3 minutes.

Add half of the stock, cover the pan and simmer for 6 minutes. Add the rest of the stock, bring it back to the boil and then put in the cabbage. Continue to cook on medium heat for 6 more minutes. Taste and add the tamarind water and fish sauce.

Put the cod fillets in this sauce and simmer for a further 3–4 minutes. Remove from the heat, put in the mint leaves and cover for 4 minutes.

Serve the curry still hot, with plain boiled rice or Coconut Rice (page 147).

Note: This dish is often served with some of the cabbage, raw and shredded, on a separate plate, for people to help themselves and eat as a salad. If you like raw cabbage, I recommend this. You can still put the rest of the cabbage into the curry to be cooked.

salads

Looking at current restaurant menus in London,
New York, or Sydney, I sometimes get the feeling
that almost any dish can be a salad if the chef
chooses to call it one. This is an illusion, of course
– a salad is a salad, and the word refers to more
or less the same kind of dish the world over.
Its place and function in the meal, however, are
somewhat different in Southeast Asia from what
they are in the West. I don't think it would ever
occur to an Asian, if he or she had spent all their
life in their home town, to serve a salad at the
beginning of the meal, still less at the almost-end,
just before the dessert. We don't limit our salads
to any particular role, any more than you would
confine them to a few conventional ingredients.
The salads in this section are especially suitable
for starters, but you can equally well regard them,
as we would in Asia, as snacks, one-dish meals
or accompaniments to the main course. And they
will always be important parts of any buffet.

avocado, orange and beetroot salad

This is a new style of salad I have created especially for this book. Avocados grow well in the tropics, as, of course, do oranges. I have introduced beetroot to my Southeast Asian cooking because I like it and because it goes well with avocado and orange as an accompaniment to duck or pork curries.

for 4–6

4 uncooked beetroot
3–4 oranges
2 ripe avocados
1 tbsp lemon or lime juice
4–5 tbsp Thai Piquant Dressing (page 158)
115 g / 4 oz rocket leaves
60 g / 2 oz coriander leaves
3 spring onions, cut into rounds

Preheat the oven to 160ºC / 325ºF / Gas 3. Scrub the beetroot, wash and dry with paper towel. Cut each in half. Put all the halves on two thicknesses of foil, fold the foil over and fold the edges to seal them, so that you have a double-wrapped, loosely-packed parcel. Put it in the oven for 45–60 minutes.

Open up the parcel, transfer the beetroot to a large glass bowl and leave it to cool. When cool, cut each half into 3 or 4 slices.

Peel and segment the oranges, making sure that all the juice is saved in the bowl with the segments. Peel and halve the avocados, remove the stones and cut the flesh into slices about the same size as the orange segments. Add these to the oranges in the bowl, then add the lemon or lime juice.

When the beetroot halves are cold, add these to the orange and avocado. Pour the Thai Piquant Dressing over all, and mix in the rocket and coriander leaves and the spring onions. Serve at room temperature, not chilled.

salad of beansprouts, cucumber and carrots

This salad has long been familiar in Southeast Asia as a side dish to refresh your palate when you are eating a well-spiced hot meal with plenty of chillies. I am certain it will be popular anywhere for the crunch of the vegetables and the sweet-and-sour tang of the dressing. Don't be tempted to use lemon juice or exotically flavoured vinegar here; only white distilled malt vinegar is appropriate.

for 6-8

1 cucumber, peeled
4–6 carrots, peeled
225 g / 8 oz beansprouts

for the dressing
115 ml / 4 fl oz white distilled vinegar
1 tsp salt
4 tbsp warm water
2 shallots, thinly sliced
1–2 red bird's-eye chilli(es), deseeded and finely chopped, or ⅛ tsp cayenne pepper
2 tsp caster sugar, or more to taste

Cut the cucumber in half lengthwise and scrape out the seeds. Slice it into thin half-moon shapes. Cut the carrots into tiny sticks.

Make the dressing: in a glass bowl, mix all the ingredients and stir until the sugar is dissolved. Taste and adjust the seasoning.

Add the beansprouts, cucumber and carrots to the dressing and combine everything well. Leave the salad at room temperature for at least 30 minutes before serving. It can be refrigerated for up to 48 hours, but should be served at room temperature.

mixed vegetable salad with peanut

sauce *In Indonesia and Malaysia this salad is called* gado-gado. *The dictionary will tell you that this literally means 'a random mix', though* gado-gado *has long since become a favourite, almost a national dish, in both countries, with the result that there is an established combination of vegetables and garnishes, soft-textured (usually hard-boiled eggs and fried tofu) and crisp (such as crisp-fried shallots and prawn crackers). This standard combination is indeed delicious, and all I can do is to suggest that its presentation be given a new look.*

**for 4-6 as a side salad
or for 2-3 as a vegetarian
one-dish meal**

**1 sweet potato, peeled and cubed
225 g / 8 oz Thai asparagus
or French beans
3 small pak choy, quartered lengthwise
115 g / 4 oz beansprouts
about 300 ml / ½ pint
Peanut Sauce (page 159)
2 hard-boiled eggs, quartered
115–150 g / 4–5 oz watercress
1 cucumber, peeled and cut into
ribbons with a potato peeler
2 carrots, peeled and cut into
ribbons with a potato peeler
1 tbsp Crisp-fried Shallots (page 170)
krupuk (prawn crackers), to serve**

for the lime juice dressing
**2 tbsp hot water
juice of 1 lime
¼ tsp salt
½ tsp sugar
1 tsp finely chopped inner parts
of a lemon grass stalk**

Cook the vegetables separately: cubed sweet potato for 8–10 minutes, French beans for 4 minutes, fine Thai asparagus for 2 minutes, pak choy for 2 minutes, beansprouts for 1 minute. Drain each vegetable thoroughly in a colander, then put them all together in a bowl and toss them in the Peanut Sauce. Add the quartered eggs.

Make the lime juice dressing by mixing all the ingredients in a bowl.

To serve, line a serving platter with the watercress. Toss the cucumber and carrot ribbons in the lime juice dressing. Pile the cooked vegetables, now dressed in the sauce, high on top of the watercress. Then arrange the dressed cucumber and carrot ribbons on top of the cooked vegetables and scatter the crisp-fried shallots over all. Serve at room temperature with prawn crackers on the side.

asinan Jakarta

This is an Indonesian salad of raw vegetables and fruit. I am not sure why it is called after the city of Jakarta, when the original (or at any rate the best-known) version comes from Bogor, to the south. Variations occur in other parts of Southeast Asia, for example in Thailand and Myanmar, where roughly chopped roasted peanuts are important for adding flavour and texture. It would commonly be sold as street food, at one time wrapped in banana leaf but now much more likely to be found in a plastic container. My new wave version is less hot and less sweet than is traditional.

*Indonesians prefer **shrimp paste** to fish sauce as a flavouring. A much more concentrated product, it can be bought in Oriental stores as a solid paste in carefully wrapped blocks, usually labelled* balachan, blachen *or* trassie; *the Indonesian name for it is* terasi. *It has a very strong smell and flavour, so don't use more than the recipe specifies, and keep it in an airtight container (it stays good for years). Most recipes require it to be roasted first. The best way to do this is to cut a few slices from the block, each about 6mm / ¼ inch thick, and cut each of these into 4 squares. Roast the squares on foil in a moderate oven or a frying pan for about 5 minutes. This creates a powerful odour, which fortunately does not hang around for long; I love it, but it does take people aback if they're not expecting it.*

for 4–6

1 cucumber, peeled
2–3 medium carrots, peeled
2 hard apples
2 small yam beans (page 15) or unripe pears
1 small pineapple, peeled and cored (optional)
115 g / 4 oz beansprouts, cleaned
115 g / 4 oz white cabbage, finely shredded
60 g / 2 oz Chinese cabbage, finely shredded

for the dressing
60 g / 2 oz brown sugar
1 tbsp caster sugar
1 tsp fried or grilled shrimp paste (see above)
2 tbsp dried shrimps (page 164)
3–5 bird's-eye chillies, or 2 small dried red chillies
1 large red chilli, deseeded and chopped
175 ml / 6 fl oz distilled malt vinegar
1 tsp salt

for the garnish
85 g / 3 oz peanuts, fried or roasted
prawn crackers
some mixed lettuce leaves

Well ahead, cut the cucumber and carrots into matchsticks, taking care not to make them too small. Slice the apples and pears not too thinly (if using yam beans, peel them first) and cut the pineapple, if using, into small pieces.

Make the dressing: in a small saucepan, dissolve the brown sugar in 4 tablespoons of water over a gentle heat. Transfer this to a large glass bowl and set aside. Put the rest of the ingredients for the dressing into a blender and blend, but not too smoothly. Add this to the bowl, stir to mix well and adjust the seasoning.

Mix all the salad ingredients in the dressing and leave to stand for a few hours or overnight in the fridge or a cool place.

Just before serving, transfer the salad mixture to a large platter, garnish with the peanuts and prawn crackers, and arrange the lettuce leaves around the edge of the platter.

roasted vegetable salad with egg noodles

When I was a small girl in Sumatra, and later in Java, I never knew of anyone having an oven. Even today, they are not often seen, except in middle-class households in the cities. For most Southeast Asians, roasting still means grilling over charcoal or the embers of a wood fire, out of doors. It is no wonder that satays – of meat, fish, shellfish or vegetables – are regarded as everyday food, or that our favourite snacks were grilled corn cobs from either our own kitchen or the nearest street vendor. Nowadays I prefer to roast my vegetables for this salad in the oven, then finish them off on the grill. In this way, I need very little time for last-minute preparation before serving.

for 4-6 as a one-bowl lunch

2 aubergines, quartered lengthwise

2 whole sweetcorn (maize) cobs

2 red peppers

2 yellow peppers

about 500 g / 1 lb peeled pumpkin, without seeds, cut into 8 wedges

2–3 tomatoes, skinned and roughly chopped

2–3 tbsp groundnut or olive oil

225–350 g / 8–12 oz dried egg noodles

salt

for the dressing

2 tbsp finely chopped spring onions

2 tsp finely chopped ginger root

2 tbsp chopped coriander or flat-leaf parsley

2 kaffir lime leaves or other citrus leaves, finely shredded

2–4 bird's-eye chillies, finely chopped

juice of 4 lemons

2–3 tbsp fish sauce (nam pla) or light soy sauce

1–2 tsp brown sugar

¼ tsp salt

4 tbsp hot water

2 tbsp groundnut or avocado oil

Preheat the oven to 180ºC / 350ºF / Gas 4. Brush all the vegetables except the tomatoes with groundnut or olive oil and roast on a rack for 15–20 minutes.

While the vegetables are still in the oven, boil the noodles in lightly salted water for 3 minutes only. Drain in a colander and run cold water over them to stop them cooking. Leave to drain.

Then grill the roasted vegetables in a ridged grill pan or barbecue them, turning them often, until they are slightly charred. You may have to do this in batches.

Meanwhile, make the dressing by mixing all the ingredients in a large glass bowl.

When ready to serve, put the aubergines and the pumpkin pieces into the bowl with the dressing. Peel the peppers, then cut each into 4–6 strips, taking care to catch all the juice from them as you do so. Strain this juice through a sieve into the bowl with the dressing. Shave the corn kernels from the cobs with a small knife, and mix them with the other vegetables. Finally, add the noodles (cutting them into short pieces with scissors, if you wish) and the tomatoes. Taste, add salt if necessary, mix well and serve at room temperature.

beancurd cake and bitter cucumber salad with lime and lemon grass dressing

Beancurd, or tofu, is generally regarded as bland, which it certainly is in its raw state. My new way with it is to make it into a spicy tofu cake, then dress it with contrasting tastes, bitter and sour, and a sprinkling of chopped chillies. This salad makes an interesting starter, or a vegetarian main course to accompany pasta with Red Pepper and Tomato Sauce (page 163).

for 4

675–900 g / 1½–2 lb Chinese-style tofu or long-life Japanese cotton tofu
3 tbsp groundnut oil
6–8 fresh shiitake mushrooms, diced
3 tbsp chopped spring onions
¼ tsp cayenne pepper
1 tsp ground coriander seeds
1 tsp salt, or a little more to taste
1 egg
2–3 tbsp plain flour
2–4 red bird's-eye chillies, deseeded and finely chopped, to garnish

for the salad
1 bitter cucumber (bitter gourd, page 98)
2 tbsp groundnut oil
3 shallots, thinly sliced

for the dressing
juice of 1–2 lime(s)
2 tsp finely chopped inner parts of lemon grass stalk.
1 tsp caster sugar

Roughly chop the tofu, then wrap it in muslin and squeeze out excess water. Put the tofu in a bowl and mash it with the back of a spoon.

Heat 1 tablespoon of the oil in a saucepan, add the diced shiitake and stir for a minute or two. Then add the spring onions, cayenne pepper and ground coriander. Stir again, then add the mashed tofu and salt. Turn off the heat, but continue stirring the mixture until all ingredients are well blended. Leave to cool. When the mixture is cold, add the egg and stir well again, so that the egg will bind the mixture when fried.

Prepare the salad: cut the bitter cucumber in half lengthwise and, with a teaspoon, scoop out the seeds together with the white membrane to which they are attached (these are the really bitter parts). Then slice the two halves thinly into half-moon shapes. Put these in a colander and sprinkle them with salt. Rub the salt in well and leave to drain for 30 minutes. Rinse under cold running water.

Heat the groundnut oil in a frying pan and fry the shallots until they just start to colour. Add the bitter cucumber and stir-fry for 3–4 minutes, adding some salt if necessary.

Make the dressing: in a small bowl, mix the lime juice, lemon grass and sugar, then mix in the bitter cucumber and the shallots.

Divide the tofu mixture into 4 and shape each into a cake. Spread the flour on a flat plate or tray. Coat the tofu cakes with the flour and fry them in the remaining oil, 2 at a time, for about 5 minutes on each side, turning them once.

Serve hot, with portions of bitter cucumber and dressing arranged on top of each tofu cake. Garnish with chopped red chillies.

Thai asparagus and squid salad *This is based on the well-known Thai squid salad, yam pla muek. The miniature asparagus which I use can be bought in most supermarkets in the West nowadays; it really does come from Thailand, and is much smaller and more slender than most of the full-size asparagus grown in Europe and North America. Wild asparagus is a good alternative, if you can get it.*

450–500 g / about 1 lb baby squid,
without tentacles, cleaned and
each cut into 4 lengthwise
3 tbsp groundnut oil
½ tsp salt
1 garlic clove, crushed
450 g / 1 lb thin Thai asparagus

for the dressing
2 tbsp fresh lime juice
2 tsp caster sugar
2 tsp rice vinegar
1–4 bird's-eye chillies, finely chopped
2 shallots, finely chopped
2 garlic cloves, finely chopped
2 tbsp fish sauce (nam pla)
a handful of coriander leaves

to garnish
2 tbsp groundnut oil
3 shallots, thinly sliced
2 large red chillies, deseeded
and thinly sliced at an angle

Put the squid pieces into a glass bowl. Add the oil, salt and garlic, and mix well by hand so that every piece of squid is coated with the mixture. Set aside.

Make the dressing by mixing all the ingredients in another (large) glass bowl.

Cook the garnishes: heat the oil in a frying pan and stir-fry the shallots and chillies for 2 minutes, adding a pinch of salt as you do so. Set aside.

Blanch the asparagus in lightly salted boiling water for 1 minute only. Drain and mix while still hot into the bowl with the dressing.

Heat a non-stick frying pan on medium heat. When hot, put the marinated squid into the pan and stir for 1 minute. Increase the heat, shake the pan, and stir the squid again for another 30 seconds. Turn off the heat and cover the pan tightly. Leave it covered for 2 minutes.

Transfer the contents of the pan, while still warm, into the bowl with the dressing. Mix well and serve at room temperature, scattering the garnishes over all.

watercress, steamed cod and boiled
egg salad
No region of Asia can claim this combination of ingredients as its local speciality; this is simply a new way of using a curry paste as a salad dressing.

for 4
4 cod fillets, each weighing
125–150 g / 4–5 oz
½ tsp salt
225–350 g / 8–12 oz watercress sprigs
or other greens
4 hard-boiled eggs, shelled
2 tbsp chopped chives

for the dressing
6 tbsp curry paste (choose whichever
one you like from pages 166–8)
3 tbsp Greek-style plain yoghurt

Rub the cod fillets all over with the salt, put on a suitable plate and steam for 2–3 minutes.

Make the dressing: whisk the curry paste and yoghurt in a saucepan with 5 tablespoons of water until well mixed. Heat this mixture slowly until it boils, then stir it with a wooden spoon. Continue simmering for 2 minutes.

Add the cod fillets, and turn them over in the dressing so that they are well coated with it. Cover the pan, turn the heat off and leave the pan covered until the fish and the dressing are cold.

Transfer the cod and the dressing to a serving bowl. Add the watercress or other greens. Quarter the eggs and add them as well. Toss the whole salad, but carefully. Serve at room temperature, as suggested above, sprinkled with chopped chives.

kinilaw of salmon and sea bass *I started to learn*

about kinilaw *from a book, entitled* Kinilaw: A Philippine Cuisine of Freshness, *by two distinguished food writers from the Philippines, Edilberto Alegre and my good friend Doreen Fernandez. In the book they explain that 'kinilaw', as the name of a dish, indicates meat, fish or vegetables cooked not on the stove but by 'liquid fire', that is vinegar or other souring agents. In this respect it obviously takes after South American* ceviche *and can be compared with Japanese* sashimi.

The Filipinos would use local river fish for this dish, but I like to make it with a mixture of salmon and sea bass because it tastes so good and looks quite spectacular. Needless to say, whatever is to be 'cooked' in this way must indeed be very fresh. A good alternative to salmon, if you are lucky enough have a trout farm within reach, is freshly caught rainbow trout. If you want vegetables to go with the fish, put into the mix very thin slices of cucumber, or carambola, mango or papaya.

There are many varieties of small, green, sour citrus fruits, valued in Southeast Asia precisely for their sourness. Most countries of the region have wonderfully thirst-quenching drinks based on the juice of these, with water, ice and sometimes a good deal of sugar: air jeruk *in Indonesia, kalamansi juice in the Philippines. The kalamansi is a Filipino lime variety. From the cook's point of view, all varieties of lime are interchangeable.*

for 4–6 as a starter

500 g / about 1 lb very fresh thin slices of salmon (preferably wild) or rainbow trout
500 g / about 1 lb very fresh thin slices of sea bass

for the marinade
2 tbsp kalamansi (tiny Philippines citrus fruits) juice, or lime or lemon juice
2 tbsp rice vinegar
2 small shallots, very thinly sliced
2.5 cm / 1 in piece of peeled ginger root, very thinly sliced, then cut into tiny sticks
1–3 bird's-eye chillies, finely chopped
½ –1 tsp fine sea salt

Make the marinade by combining all the ingredients in a bowl.

Arrange slices of alternating fish on a platter so that they do not overlap each other and carefully pour the mix all over them. In a very short time, you will see the translucent flesh become opaque. The kinilaw is now ready. Serve immediately.

As a variation, you can add finely chopped herbs of your choice to the vinegar mix. Leave out the chillies, if you wish, and add a tiny amount of sugar.

seafood salad with avocado *Since we all travel such a lot now, and food travels faster than any of us, it is not surprising to find Mexican guacamole in Southeast Asia, and a lot of Asians who now realize that avocado is good in savoury dishes too.*

for 2 as a one-dish light meal, or 4 as a starter

225 ml / 8 fl oz thick coconut milk
2 tbsp lemon juice
1 tsp salt
225 g / 8 oz halibut steaks
8–12 large uncooked king prawns, shells removed
225 g / 8 oz baby squid, cleaned and halved
1–2 ripe avocados (½ avocado per portion)
1 tsp soy sauce
1 tsp mirin (Japanese rice wine)
juice of 1 lemon
a pinch of salt
a good selection of salad leaves, enough for 2 or 4 people

for the avocado dressing
3 tbsp fresh lemon juice
1 tsp sugar
½ tsp salt
¼ tsp cayenne pepper
2 garlic cloves, finely chopped
2 tbsp chopped coriander leaves
1 large ripe avocado

Put the coconut milk, lemon juice and salt in a shallow saucepan. Heat this until just boiling. Add the fish, prawns and squid, and poach them for 2 minutes. Turn off the heat, cover the pan and allow the seafood to cook for 2 more minutes. Drain in a colander and leave to get cold.

Make the dressing: mix all the ingredients except the avocado in a glass bowl. Peel the avocado, remove the stone, dice the flesh and put the cubes immediately into the dressing. Mix well and add the seafood.

Peel and halve the other avocado(s) for the salad, then slice each half lengthwise into 4 or 5 slices. Mix the soy sauce, mirin, lemon juice and salt in a bowl, and dip the avocado slices into this mixture to prevent discoloration.

To serve: divide the salad leaves among 2 or 4 plates. Arrange the slices of each half-avocado in a fan on top of each plate of salad. Finally, arrange equal portions of seafood on each plate, either on top of the salad or at the side. Serve at room temperature.

salad of steamed assorted fish with soy, ginger and green onion dressing *By choosing whole small fish and steaming them whole, you will make this taste really good. Instead of serving it with a green salad, I accompany it with a salad of pink pomelo, apples and pears in a soy-ginger dressing.*

for 4

1 rainbow trout, about 675 g / 1½ lb
1 small sea bass, about 675 g / 1½ lb
½ tsp salt

for the salad
2 Cox's apples
2 large, slightly unripe pears
1 pink pomelo, peeled and segmented

for the dressing
10 cm / 4 in piece of ginger root, peeled
2 tbsp light soy sauce
4–6 spring onions, cut into thin rounds
¼ tsp cayenne pepper
2 tbsp lemon juice
1 tbsp mirin (Japanese rice wine)

First make the dressing: cut the ginger into tiny sticks, then mix these with all the other ingredients in a glass bowl.

Peel and core the apples and pears. Slice them into thin segments and put all the slices into the dressing to prevent discoloration. Pick off the skin from each segment of the pomelo, so that the juicy sacs inside break up into small groups. Put these into the dressing also. Keep everything in a cool place while you prepare the fish.

Rub the fish with the salt and steam them, side by side, for 10–12 minutes. Leave to cool. When cool enough to handle, skin them. The flesh will then flake easily and come away from the bones.

Arrange the fish on 4 plates. Divide the fruit and dressing equally and pour them over the fish. Serve at room temperature.

banana flower and chicken salad *This recipe is*
Khmer, from Le Royal Hotel in Phnom Penh, though I have adapted it a little to suit my
way of cooking. If you can't get banana flowers, use palm hearts instead.

for 4-6 small portions

2 chicken breasts, with skin and the bone
1 fresh banana flower
2 tbsp lime juice
1 tsp rice vinegar
1 tsp fine sea salt
endive or lollo rosso leaves, to serve

for the dressing
1 large red chilli, deseeded and chopped
2 garlic cloves, chopped
1 tsp chopped ginger
1 tsp chopped Chinese keys
(optional, page 109)
1 tsp fried shrimp paste (page 122)
1 tbsp tamarind water (page 164)
2 tbsp sunflower or groundnut oil
1 tsp fish sauce (nam pla or nuoc mam)
2 tsp grated palm or coconut sugar

to garnish
2 shallots, thinly sliced at an angle
2 red chillies, deseeded and thinly sliced
slices of fresh lime

Cook the chicken breasts in lightly salted water to cover for 15 minutes. Remove them from the stock and leave to cool. Meanwhile, remove the two outer layers of hard reddish-purple leaves from the banana flower and discard, then halve the interior.

When the chicken is cold, remove skin and bones and return these to the stock pot. Bring the stock to the boil again and, when boiling, add the halved banana flower, half the lime juice, the vinegar and salt. Simmer for 10 minutes. Remove the banana flower from the stock and leave it to cool. Discard the stock, which by now has taken the bitterness from the flower.

Slice the cooked banana flower into julienne strips. Do the same with the chicken breast meat. Set aside.

Make the dressing by putting all the ingredients in a blender and blending until smooth. Transfer to a saucepan and cook, stirring often, for 5–6 minutes. Taste and adjust the seasoning with salt, pepper and lime juice, if necessary.

Now add the julienned banana flower and chicken breast meat. Stir them around on a low heat for a minute or two, then remove from the heat and let them cool.

To serve: arrange the endive or lollo rosso leaves on a platter and place the cold mixture on top. Garnish with slices of shallots, chillies and lime. Serve at room temperature.

some asian herbs

The herbs here are as various as their origins, and they play surprisingly diverse roles in different areas of Asia.

Basil (*Ocimum basilicum* and *O. gratissimum* or *sanctum*), see page 39.

Chinese chives (*Allium tuberosum*) ❹ These originated as a wild herb in China and they are in fact a kind of onion, though it is the leaves and flowers that are eaten. Bunched for sale, they can look like large chives, though when they are grown commercially the plants are usually earthed-up like celery to make the lower parts of the stems white. The leaves, unlike those of 'ordinary' chives and onions, are solid and more or less flat, and the mildly garlicky flavour of the flowers makes them suitable for salads. They are of course excellent for seasoning, and leaves, buds and flowers can all be cooked. Fresh Chinese chives will keep for several days in plastic bags in the fridge salad compartment, and can be frozen.

Coriander (*Coriandrum sativum*) ❺ This excellent herb and spice originated somewhere around the eastern Mediterranean, but it was taken long ago to China and India and thence to Africa and Southeast Asia. The roots, the leaves and the ripe seeds are all useful in cooking, but are not all used in every cuisine. For example, in Indonesia we use only the seeds, whole or ground; most people there don't like the smell or flavour of the leaves. The Thais, however, use the leaves and the roots, which add their own special flavour to the dish. Coriander leaves and seeds can be bought almost anywhere; finding roots is not so easy in countries where they are trimmed off and thrown away. Many Thai stores buy their coriander leaves direct from Thailand, and there are usually a few stems with roots or root fragments still attached. Buy these when you see them; you can freeze the roots until needed.

Kaffir lime (*Citrus hystrix*) ❸ This small tree, with shiny, dark pointed green leaves, bears fruit that look like small green lemons, with noticeably wrinkled skins. Leaves and fruit are imported into Britain from Thailand and are usually available in Thai shops and some supermarkets. The juice (what there is) and rind, but more especially the leaves, are used in cooking; they give a characteristic citrusy flavour, and the juice, as one would expect, is particularly sour. Curry leaves or even bay leaves are just about acceptable as substitutes if the real thing cannot be found. Bay leaves are stronger and one bay leaf will replace 2–3 kaffir lime leaves.

Lemon grass (*Cymbopogon citratus*) ❷, see page 78.

Pandanus (*Pandanus odorus*) ❶, see page 186.

Thai beef salad

*Of all the Southeast Asian cuisines, I find Thai comes up with the most delicious salads, or at any rate the salads that appeal most to Western tastes. The two that are probably best known, both in the East and in the West, are this beef salad (*yam neua*) and the squid salad (*yam pla muek*), a version of which you'll find on pages 126–7. For this, I share the preference of the Thais for beef that is not too pink, so my choice is rump steak, or slices of roasted fore rib.*

for 4 as a one-dish lunch (allow 115–175 g / 4-6 oz of cooked beef per person)

675 g / 1½ lb (or a little more) rump steak (in one or two pieces) or slices of roasted rib of beef coarse sea salt and freshly ground black pepper

for the dressing
3 tbsp fresh lime juice
2 tbsp fish sauce (nam pla)
1 tbsp sugar
3 tbsp warm water
2–4 bird's-eye chillies, deseeded and finely chopped
1 tsp finely chopped fresh galangal (page 109, optional)
1 tsp chopped lemon grass (soft inner part only)
a handful of coriander leaves, roughly chopped, plus more whole leaves to garnish
Crisp-fried Shallots (page 170), to garnish

for the salad
1–2 Cos lettuce(s), the inner leaves only
1 cucumber, peeled then cut into ribbons with a potato peeler
2 carrots, peeled then cut into ribbons with a potato peeler
a handful of mint leaves
some rocket or lamb's lettuce leaves (optional)

Make the dressing by mixing all the ingredients in a glass bowl.

If using rump steak, rub it all over with coarse sea salt and freshly ground pepper. Grill the rump steak to your preference: it should be medium-rare or a little more. Slice it thinly across the grain.

While it is still warm, and about 10–15 minutes before you are ready to serve, put the slices into the bowl with the dressing. If using sliced roasted beef, put these into the dressing.

Arrange the salad mixture on a serving platter, place the beef slices on top and pour the dressing over all. Garnish with coriander leaves and Crisp-fried Shallots. Serve at room temperature. Alternatively, the salad mixture can be divided among individual plates (preferably large ones, to make the best effect) and arranged attractively, with the slices of beef on top. Or, if you are using large slices of roasted beef, you can roll these to contain some of the salad.

rice, noodles and pulses

Cooking with these basic foods is infinitely rewarding. They can be the foundations for any meal, from the simplest to the most elaborate; think of the billions of daily breakfasts, lunches and dinners around the world that have at least one of these as a principal element. Rice and noodles – the starches – will take up something of the flavour of any sauce or liquid with which they come in contact, while the legumes – beans, peas and, above all, lentils – add their own flavours to the dish without losing their identity and texture. In most Asian countries, rice is indeed the real staple. Don't be surprised if you are offered plain boiled rice with a fried noodle dish as an accompaniment. Lentils, or dhal, are definitely not a staple in Southeast Asia, simply a side dish. In most Asian countries people still eat rice three times a day. Even a substantial meal of meat or poultry or fish, with vegetables (including potatoes), is still considered just a snack if there is no rice.

laksa lemak

The original rice noodle soup with coconut milk, this classic Malaysian one-bowl meal, delicious and satisfying as it is, is rapidly becoming an international favourite, and it's easy to understand why. It is important, however, to use the right ingredients and to cook them the right way, without skimping or cutting corners. Some of the best laksa *I've ever had were in Asian food courts in Australia, where crowds of office workers gathered for lunch and the staff must have been cooking huge quantities, but there was no loss of quality. 'Laksa' means 'rice vermicelli', 'lemak' means 'fat' or 'rich' – in this case, it refers to the rich flavour of the coconut milk. It's important, therefore, to have the right paste and the right consistency for this, but you can use whatever noodles you like.*

for 4 as a one-bowl meal

1.1 litres / 2 pt chicken stock (page 174)
2 chicken breasts
225–350 g / 8–12 oz rice vermicelli, rice sticks, or egg noodles
1 recipe quantity Laksa Paste (page 169)
16 raw king prawns, heads removed and deveined
1 can (280 ml / 10 fl oz) coconut milk
salt and pepper

to garnish
115–175 g / 4–6 oz fried tofu, thinly sliced
115 g / 4 oz beansprouts
2 tbsp chopped spring onions
a handful of flat-leaf parsley
2 tbsp Crisp-fried Shallots (page 170)

In a large pan, bring the stock to the boil. Cook the chicken breasts in the simmering stock for 10 minutes. Remove and leave to cool slightly. When cool enough to handle, slice thinly.

While the chicken is poaching, soak the rice vermicelli in hot water for 5 minutes, or cook the rice sticks or egg noodles in boiling water, 2–3 minutes for rice sticks and 3 minutes for egg noodles. Refresh all of them under cold running water and drain in a colander.

Bring the stock back to the boil, add the laksa paste and simmer for 5 minutes. Add the prawns, increase the heat and cook the prawns for 2 minutes only. With a slotted spoon, remove the prawns from the stock and put them in a bowl. Set aside.

Continue cooking the broth on a medium heat for a few minutes more, then add the coconut milk and chicken slices. Cook over a medium heat, stirring often, for 15 minutes. Taste and adjust the seasoning.

Put the noodles in a colander and pour boiling water from the kettle over them to reheat them. Drain well. Divide the noodles and the garnishes among 4 large soup bowls. Put equal numbers of prawns on top and ladle the hot soup with the chicken into the bowls. Serve at once, very hot.

Singapore rice sticks

There is nothing new in this recipe, but I include it because it is one of the best-known dishes all around the Pacific Rim, and anyone with a serious interest in cooking Asian food simply has to know it. The best that I have ever eaten was in Singapore, many years ago. It was made with wide ribbon rice sticks, plenty of huge tiger prawns and thin slices of pork, slightly charred at the edges from when the noodles, in the final seconds of cooking, were tossed in the chef's steel wok over ferocious heat before being tipped into a large white serving bowl.

for 4

450 g / 1 lb wide ribbon rice sticks
2 carrots, thinly sliced
4 baby pak choy, halved lengthwise
2 tbsp groundnut oil
4 shallots, thinly sliced
4 garlic cloves, thinly sliced
2 tsp chopped ginger
6 tbsp Laksa Paste (page 169)
8 large tiger prawns, heads removed, shelled and deveined
4 large tiger prawns, with heads and in the shell, legs removed
175 g / 6 oz loin of pork, thinly sliced (or the best ham you can get, sliced)
1–2 tbsp light soy sauce
3 large tomatoes, skinned, deseeded and chopped
6 spring onions, cut into 2 cm / ¾ in pieces

Cook the rice sticks for 3 minutes in boiling water. Refresh under cold running water and drain in a colander. Blanch the carrots for 1 minute, refresh and drain. Blanch the pak choy for 2 minutes, refresh and drain.

In a wok, heat the oil and fry the shallots, garlic and ginger for 2–3 minutes. When just starting to colour, add the laksa paste. Turn the heat up, stir the paste and, when very hot, add the prawns, including those on their shells. Stir continuously on a high heat for 3 minutes, then turn the heat off. Take out the prawns, leaving as much of the paste as possible in the wok. Set them aside.

Heat the wok again and, when the paste is hot, stir in the pork or ham, ensuring it is well coated with the paste, about 4 minutes. Add the carrots, pak choy, soy sauce, tomatoes and spring onions. Stir-fry for 2 minutes. Meanwhile, put a kettleful of water to heat and preheat a hot grill or ridged griddle pan.

Heat the rice sticks in the colander by pouring the kettleful of boiling water over them. Drain well, add to the hot paste and toss for 1 minute.

Put the shelled prawns back in the wok and toss and stir everything on high heat for another minute. Further cook the prawns with heads and shells, under the grill or on the ridged griddle pan, for 1–2 minutes on each side. Serve straight away, putting a heads-on prawn on each plate as a garnish.

parsleyed soba noodles with tofu and avocado tempura
I was inspired by my friend Chef Beh Kim Un to use avocado as described here. At Shakahari, one of the restaurants he and John Dunham own in Melbourne, my favourite dish is 'Absolute Avocado'. If you go there, don't miss it.

for 4

225 g / 8 oz soba noodles
1–2 ripe avocado(s)
groundnut oil, for deep-frying
1 block (about 450 g / 1 lb) of Chinese-style tofu, cut into 16 cubes
225 g / 8 oz flat-leaf parsley
60 g / 2 oz butter
¼ tsp salt

for the spiced tempura batter
2 egg yolks
350 ml / 12 fl oz iced water
1 tsp ground coriander
¼ tsp cayenne pepper
a large pinch of freshly grated nutmeg
¼ tsp salt
275–350 g / 10–12 oz plain flour

Cook the noodles in boiling water for 4–5 minutes, turning them with a wooden spoon several times. Tip into a colander and hold them under cold running water, turning them over by hand until they are cold. Leave to drain.

Preheat the oven to 100°C / 210°F / Gas ¼ and put a kettleful of water to heat. Make the batter: whisk the egg yolks lightly in a bowl, adding the iced water a little at a time. Mix the spices and salt with the flour, sift into the water and egg, and whisk to blend. Don't beat smooth; it is should be a bit lumpy.

Peel the avocado(s), cut them in half and stone. Cut each half across into 6–8 slices and put at once into the batter. Don't put the tofu in the batter. Heat the oil in a wok or deep-fryer (see page 63) and fry the avocado, 4–6 slices at a time, for about 2 minutes, turning once. Removed with a slotted spoon and drain on kitchen paper. Fry the tofu, dipping each piece in batter just as it goes in the oil. Fry as the avocado. Keep the fried avocado and tofu warm in the oven.

Reheat the noodles with hot water from the kettle. Chop most of the parsley. In a wok, heat the butter until melted and hot. Add the chopped parsley and salt, stir and add the noodles. Stir for 1–2 minutes. Transfer to a serving bowl, and arrange the tempura on top. Serve garnished with the remaining parsley.

rice sticks with duck curry and spinach

crisps *You can make this as here, with only a few spices, or with any of the curry pastes described on pages 166–8. I have simplified the method considerably and shortened the cooking time. The spinach crisps give a wonderful texture contrast.*

for 4-6 as a main course

350 ml / 12 fl oz coconut milk
350–450 g / 12–16 oz rice sticks
6 whole duck breast fillets, with skin
coarse sea salt
2 tsp fish sauce (nam pla, optional)
18–24 whole spinach leaves,
patted dry with kitchen paper
groundnut or sunflower oil,
for frying and deep-frying

for the curry paste
2 onions, chopped
2 bird's-eye chillies, chopped
1 large sweet pepper (preferably
Romano), deseeded and chopped
6 garlic cloves, chopped
2 tsp chopped ginger root
2 tsp coriander seeds, roughly crushed
juice of 1 orange
juice of 1 lemon
2 kaffir lime leaves, roughly shredded
1 tsp salt
2 tbsp groundnut oil

for the batter
2 candlenuts, chopped
1 garlic clove, chopped
115 g / 4 oz rice powder
1 tsp salt
1–2 tsp ground coriander

First make the curry paste: put all the ingredients in a blender and blend until smooth. Transfer to a pan, bring to the boil and simmer, covered, for 6–8 minutes, stirring from time to time.

In another pan, heat the coconut milk with 175 ml / 6 fl oz water. Leave to simmer, uncovered, for 5 minutes.

Make the batter for the spinach crisps: put 4 tablespoons of water in a blender with the chopped candlenuts and garlic. Blend for a few seconds so that the nuts and garlic are well mixed into the water. Transfer this cloudy liquid to a glass bowl, add 150 ml / ¼ pint more water and the remaining ingredients, then whisk until well mixed, so that you have a thick but runny batter.

Cook the rice sticks in boiling water for 2–3 minutes until tender and then drain and refresh under cold water. Drain again in a colander and set aside.

Rub the duck breast fillets all over with coarse sea salt, then rinse well (to remove any strong odours). Rub a large, preferably non-stick, pan with a little oil and place over a high heat. Put the breasts in the pan, skin side down, for 2–3 minutes. Turn over and cook for 3 minutes more, taking care they do not burn.

Add the curry paste, cover and simmer for 10–15 minutes. Add the coconut milk and continue cooking on a medium heat, this time uncovered, for 20–25 minutes. The sauce should, by now, be well reduced but not too thick. Taste, and adjust the seasoning by adding more salt or some fish sauce.

While the duck is cooking, make the spinach crisps. (You can make these earlier and store in an airtight container; they will stay crisp for up to 4 hours.) Put about 115 ml / 4 fl oz of groundnut oil in a frying pan and heat. Stir the batter and add 4 spinach leaves, making sure they are well coated with it. With a tablespoon, lift out one leaf, with a little batter clinging to it, and drop into the hot oil. Cook 3 more leaves in the same way. Work fast, because you need to have 4 leaves frying together for 1–2 minutes. When done, take them out with a slotted spoon and drain on 2 thicknesses of kitchen paper. Repeat until all the leaves have been fried. At this stage the batter is still soft.

The next step is to deep-fry the battered spinach leaves until crisp. In a wok or deep-fryer, heat oil for deep-frying to 160ºC / 320ºF and deep-fry 4 or 5 leaves at a time for about 2 minutes. Drain on kitchen paper.

To serve: reheat the sauce if necessary. Take the duck breasts from the sauce, remove the skins and slice each at an angle into 5 or 6 slices. Put back in the sauce to heat up again for 2 minutes. Heat the rice sticks by pouring boiling water over them. Divide the well-drained noodles among the plates. Then divide the slices of duck and the sauce among the plates on top of the noodles. Bring to the table and put the spinach crisps on top of each serving at the very last moment, so that they stay crisp.

venison and spiced noodles or rice sticks

Egg noodles or udon can be used for this dish, instead of rice sticks. The noodles are spiced by being mixed with the cooking sauce of the venison just before serving. For practical reasons, it is advisable to cook the venison well in advance, several hours or even a day ahead. The noodles, naturally, are cooked just before they are served. In Laos, a venison dish would be served with glutinous rice, or if with noodles then the choice would be rice sticks.

for 4–6

1.4 litres / 2½ pt thick coconut milk
5 shallots, finely chopped
4 garlic cloves, finely chopped
3 cm / 1¼ in piece of peeled ginger, finely chopped
2–4 large red chillies, deseeded and very finely chopped
1 tsp ground turmeric
1 kg / 2¼ lb venison (leg or haunch), cut into 3 cm / 1¼ in cubes
1½ tsp sea salt
3 cm / 1¼ in piece of galangal (page 109)
2–4 kaffir lime leaves
1 lemon grass stalk, cut across into halves
350–450 g / 12–16 oz noodles or rice sticks, pre-cooked as described on page 138) and drained
2 tbsp chopped spring onions, to garnish

Put all the ingredients except the noodles and spring onions in a large, heavy-based pan. Bring to the boil on a medium heat and cook the venison, uncovered, for 45 minutes, boiling all the time. The coconut milk will reduce in quantity by about half.

Lower the heat a little and continue cooking for 30 minutes, stirring the contents of the pan quite often to prevent things sticking to the bottom. The sauce will by now be quite thick. Taste it and add more salt if necessary.

Bring a kettleful of water to the boil. Remove and discard the galangal, lime leaves and lemon grass before serving. Transfer the meat and sauce to a serving bowl and garnish with chopped spring onion. (Refrigerate if the dish is to be served the next day.)

Reheat the noodles by putting them in a colander and pouring the kettleful of boiling water over them. Drain well and put them in another serving bowl. Heat the venison (if it has gone cold or been refrigerated) in a saucepan on a medium heat. Pour 2 ladlefuls of the hot sauce over the noodles and toss them well.

Let everyone help themselves: noodles first, then the venison and the sauce, which is quite rich. If you have any leftovers, they can be reheated and served with rice, glutinous rice or potatoes. Whether with noodles, potatoes or rice, a side salad or some cooked vegetables (beans or carrots) will always be good accompaniments.

shredded venison and rice vermicelli

salad
Shredded venison, with a sesame oil dressing, is often among the cold starters on a Chinese restaurant menu. The Laotians, too, are very fond of venison, though their deer is a smaller animal than the European type. I find that this finely shredded meat goes well with rice vermicelli as a light lunch dish. Plain boiled asparagus, particularly white asparagus when it's in season, will make the meal memorable. The important thing to remember is that the shredded venison must be dressed while the meat is still quite hot. If you can't get a hold of any venison try it with stewing beef.

for 6-8

675–900 g / 1 ½–2 lb venison
(leg or haunch), in 2 pieces
2 red onions, thinly sliced
3 tsp finely chopped ginger root
150 ml / 5 fl oz Shaohsing
wine or dry sherry
225 g / 8 oz rice vermicelli, prepared
as described on page 138 and drained

for the dressing

1 tbsp extra-virgin olive oil or walnut oil
2 tsp sesame oil
2 tbsp light soy sauce
1 garlic clove, finely chopped
1 tsp freshly ground black pepper
3 tbsp of the venison cooking juices
salt
sugar

to garnish

freshly boiled asparagus
(white or green; allow 3 stalks per
person, optional)
2 tsp roasted sesame seeds
150 g / 5 oz chopped spring onions
or Chinese chives

Bring a large pan of water to a rolling boil and plunge the two pieces of venison into the water. Leave them to boil for 3 minutes, then drain and discard the water.

Transfer the venison to a high-sided plate that will fit inside your steamer and add the onions, ginger and wine or sherry. Half-fill the bottom part of the steamer with cold water. Bring this to a rolling boil, then put the plate of venison into the steamer. Cover and steam for 40–50 minutes. Halfway through the cooking time, replenish the boiling water in the bottom of the steamer from a freshly boiled kettle.

While the venison is steaming, make the dressing by mixing all the ingredients in a glass bowl. Taste and add salt and/or sugar to taste. Set aside.

When the venison is cooked, transfer the meat to a large chopping board and slice it across the grain with a sharp knife, then cut the slices along the grain, so cutting the venison into julienne sticks. Put these into a bowl and pour two-thirds of the dressing over them. Toss to mix and coat every piece of the meat.

Re-heat the rice vermicelli by putting it in a sieve and pouring hot water over it. Drain well and cut the strands into short lengths with scissors. Put these into a bowl with the remaining dressing. Toss and arrange the noodles on a platter, then top with the dressed shredded venison and the garnishes.

Let the dish get cold, then serve when you are ready. If the dish has been prepared more than 2 or 3 hours in advance, cover the platter with cling-film and store it in the fridge, taking it out about 30 minutes before you intend to serve it.

all about rice and noodles

Most people in tropical Southeast Asia are accustomed to rice that goes quite soft and slightly sticky when cooked. In England, I always keep a large bag or two of 'Thai Fragrant' or 'Thai Jasmine' rice, which is similar to the rice we ate every day when I was a child. Long-grain basmati, or ultra-short-grain Italian varieties, are unrivalled for their various purposes but are not those I generally had in mind when writing this book.

Rice sold in supermarkets is pretty even in quality, but a lot of 'instant' or 'convenience' rice has been parboiled at the factory and this can affect the flavour. Rice milled in Europe, such as Tilda, is always of the highest quality, and generally speaking there is no market here for the low-grade products sold cheaply in Asia. If you buy imported jasmine rice in a Thai food shop, look for the AAA sign that indicates top-quality.

Rice that has been properly handled will keep for at least 3 years from harvesting, with no perceptible decline in quality, so best-by dates are not usually a problem. If you store it at home and forget about it for months, it will dry out and harden so it takes longer to cook and doesn't taste so good, but won't go bad.

How much rice should you cook? Regular rice eaters need far more than people who regard it as exotic. Two cups of rice (say, 250 g / ½ lb) boiled with 2½ cups of water, will be ample for 6–8 average Westerners; it would probably feed 4 Indonesians, or 2 who are really hungry. Leftover rice can be refrigerated and reheated next day. Don't store it too long at room temperature – after a day or so air-borne bacilli can make it toxic.

Cooking rice: If cooking rice regularly, invest in an electric rice cooker. This cooks the rice and switches itself off automatically, then switches itself on again at intervals to keep it warm. This does dry the rice out, so I unplug mine when it is cooked.

The other way to boil rice is in an ordinary pan. Proportions are the same: 2 of rice to 2½ of water. Bring to the boil (don't add salt), stir and simmer, uncovered, until the water is absorbed (about 10 minutes). To 'finish' the rice, cover with a tight-fitting lid and leave on a very low heat for 10–12 minutes. Make a pad of a cold, wet tea towel on your draining board, and put the pan on this, with the lid still firmly on. Leave to rest for 5 minutes. The cold wet cloth stops the bottom layer of rice sticking to the pan.

To check the rice is done, rub a grain between your fingers or eat a few. If the centres are noticeably harder than the outer layers, the rice needs to steam a few more minutes. Glutinous rice (which, like all rice, is totally gluten-free; 'sticky rice' is a better name) needs to be cooked for a few minutes longer.

Noodles and wrappers These are Asian forms of pasta, produced by making a dough of flour, water and salt (and sometimes egg), rolling it into thin sheets, cutting these into long, thin ribbons or other shapes, and drying. Instant noodles are now a huge industry throughout most of Asia, but, as with any pasta, high quality comes only from the best ingredients. Always buy dry noodles imported from the country where that particular type of noodle originated. From China, we get egg noodles, wonton and spring roll wrappers, and cellophane (also called glass) noodles, made from mung bean flour. Most rice noodles (i.e. made from rice flour), including rice sticks and rice – or glass – vermicelli, and rice paper wrappers, come from Thailand or Vietnam. Japanese noodles (e.g. soba noodles) must be made in Japan. Dried noodles in sealed packets can be stored for a long time, but will gradually lose flavour and texture after their best-by dates. Beware of labels stuck on Asian noodles by Western importers, as these often have erroneous instructions on how to cook the contents.

❶ left to right: basmati rice, black rice (see page 181), Thai fragrant rice; ❷ rice vermicelli; ❸ rice sticks; ❹ egg noodles; ❺ soba noodles

pad Thai with seafood

Pad Thai *simply means fried noodles, the equivalent of* chow mein *in Chinese,* bakmie goreng *in Indonesia or* mee goreng *in Malaysia. The other ingredients are different in each country and region, and as it is an all-purpose everyday dish, everyone has their own favourite variant. The basic and probably the most popular* pad Thai *is made with pork and vegetables, as described in my book* Noodles the New Way, *but here I give a seafood version using different ingredients, and the method is also different. Instead of stir-frying everything together, the seafood is cooked separately and tossed with the noodles just before serving. The basic* pad Thai *is usually garnished with chopped roasted peanuts, but I omit these here.*

for 4–6

2 tbsp groundnut oil
4 shallots, thinly sliced
2 tsp finely chopped ginger root
450 g / 1 lb baby spinach
¼ tsp cayenne pepper
1 tsp ground coriander
1 tbsp fish sauce (nam pla) or light soy sauce
½ tsp brown sugar
1 tbsp tomato purée
4 tbsp hot water
salt and pepper
350–450 g / 12–16 oz fine egg noodles or narrow-ribbon rice sticks, cooked and refreshed as described on page 138
2 tbsp chopped coriander leaves

for the seafood

225–350 g / 8–12 oz ready-cleaned small squid, cut into bite-sized pieces
2 tbsp groundnut oil
3 salmon fillets, each about 115 g / 4 oz, cut in halves
3 tuna fillets, each about 115–150 g / 4–5 oz, cut in halves
8–12 large cooked prawns in the shell, with tails but heads removed
4–6 small scallops, each cut into 2 discs
juice of 1 lemon
1 tsp sugar
¼ tsp cayenne pepper
2 tbsp fish sauce (nam pla)
2–4 garlic cloves, crushed
2 tbsp chopped creamed coconut (page 179), dissolved in 4 tbsp hot water

Sauté the squid in a little hot oil in a non-stick frying pan for 2 minutes. Drain and allow to cool slightly.

In a large bowl, mix the squid with all the other the seafood and their flavouring ingredients, making sure that all the fish, prawns etc. are well coated with them. Set aside.

When ready to eat, heat the oil in a wok and stir-fry the shallots and ginger for 2 minutes. Add the rest of the ingredients except the coriander leaves and noodles. Stir until the mixture is hot. Taste and adjust the seasoning by adding salt, pepper and more fish sauce as necessary.

Put the cooked noodles in a colander and pour boiling water from a kettle over them to re-heat them. Drain well and mix the noodles with the mixture in the wok, stirring and tossing them to mix them together.

Cook the seafood. Heat a large non-stick frying pan or saucepan. Rub the surface with a little oil. While the pan gets hotter, transfer all the seafood from the bowl to the hot pan. Shake the pan or stir the seafood gently with a non-stick spatula, taking care not to break up the slices of fish. Cover tightly and continue cooking for 1 more minute only.

Remove the pan from the heat but keep the cover on for 2 more minutes to let the seafood finish cooking. Add to the wok with the noodles, toss everything to mix all the ingredients together and serve straight away, at room temperature.

Variation: An alternative method of serving is to heat the noodles in the wok, stirring and tossing them for 2 minutes. Divide them among 4 or 6 warmed plates and arrange the seafood on top of each pile of noodles.

coconut rice

Nowhere in Asia do cooks put any salt in plain boiled or steamed rice. Salt and spices are used when one is making a pilaf or pulao, and, of course, in fried rice. Coconut rice is rice cooked in coconut milk instead of water, and you add salt to this because the salt enhances the coconut flavour.

for 6-8

450 g / 1 lb basmati or Thai fragrant rice
2 tbsp vegetable oil or clarified butter
1 tsp ground turmeric
(for yellow rice only)
1 tsp salt
600 ml / 1 pt coconut milk

If using basmati rice, first soak it in cold water for 2 hours; simply rinse Thai rice. Heat the oil or butter in a large pan and, when hot, add the turmeric, if using, and salt. Stir and add the drained rice. Stir until all the grains are coated.

Add the coconut milk and bring to the boil. Simmer, uncovered, until all the liquid has been absorbed. Then stir the rice once, lower the heat, cover tightly and leave for 10–15 minutes.

glutinous rice rolls

The hills of mainland Southeast Asia are still the home of numerous ethnic groups and tribes whose favourite food and principal food crop is glutinous rice. (Some of them are opium farmers too, but that's another story.) In northern Thailand, around Chiang Rai and Chiang Mai, I came across people cooking this rice in tubes of young green bamboo and selling it at roadside stalls; it is delicious, and a very healthy and satisfying snack when travelling. Elsewhere in Asia 'sticky rice' is cooked in banana leaves. For this recipe, however, I won't send you out in search of bamboo or bananas, but concentrate on a tasty and popular filling for your rolls. If you have a sushi mat, that will help with the rolling, but you can use plain cooking foil.

makes 3-4 rolls

450 g / 1 lb glutinous rice, rinsed
600 ml / 1 pt thick coconut milk
½ tsp salt
1 pandanus leaf, cut into 3 (optional)

for the tuna and basil filling

3 tbsp groundnut oil
115 g / 4 oz shallots, finely chopped
6 garlic cloves, finely chopped
1 tbsp finely chopped ginger root
3 red chillies, deseeded
and finely chopped
115 g / 4 oz basil, chopped
115 g / 4 oz spring onions, chopped
3 tomatoes, skinned,
deseeded and chopped
salt and pepper
450 g / 1 lb fresh tuna steak,
cubed then chopped

Cook the rice: heat the milk in a large pan until just boiling. Take off the heat and add the salt and pandan leaf, if using. Stir, add the rice, stir again, cover and leave undisturbed for 10 minutes, until all the milk has been absorbed. Transfer to a steamer and steam for 10–15 minutes. Put the rice in a large bowl.

To make the filling: heat the oil in a shallow pan or a wok and stir-fry the shallots, garlic and ginger for 5 minutes, then add the rest of the ingredients except the tuna. Add the tuna meat about 1–2 minutes before taking off the heat.

Line the sushi mat with film or foil. Spread a quarter or a third of the rice on this, pressing flat with your hand covered in foil. The rice should cover the mat evenly, except for about 5 cm / 2 in on the edge furthest from you. Put several spoonfuls of filling in the centre, then roll up the mat, taking care not to let the film or foil get inside the rice. Roll round several times on your work-top to consolidate the rice grains and make them stick together. Remove the mat and roll a few more times to make firm up. Repeat with the rest of the rice and filling.

Serve the rolls at room temperature, sliced across into thick pieces. If you refrigerate the rolls, they are easier to cut while still chilled, but don't serve them straight from the fridge; they need at least 5 hours to get back to room temperature and be ready to eat.

pork dumplings with a rich coconut sauce on sweetcorn rice

The rich coconut sauce used here is the Indonesian Sambal Goreng sauce described on page 162. 'Sweetcorn rice' may not be immediately recognizable to Indonesians of a younger generation than mine, but for my sisters and me, who were children during the Japanese occupation and the years of revolution, it was a staple food when there was not enough rice by itself to go round. Sweetcorn and coconut were added simply to give bulk, but in fact they make rather a good combination and I am reintroducing this dish as a kind of new wave pilaf. The pork dumplings also contain several other interesting ingredients.

for 6 as a one-dish meal

6–8 boneless pork chops,
with some fat, minced,
or 350 g / 12 oz minced pork
8–10 raw king prawns, shelled
and deveined, then chopped
4 garlic cloves, chopped
3 shallots, chopped
1 tsp chopped ginger
about 1½ tsp salt
1 tsp light soy sauce
½ tsp chilli oil
white of 1 egg, lightly beaten
1 tbsp lemon juice
Sambal Goreng Sauce (page 162)
60–125 g / 2–4 oz pea shoots (page 22)

for the sweetcorn rice

175 g / 6 oz white or red long-grain rice
175 g / 6 oz sweetcorn kernels
(fresh, frozen or canned)
4 tbsp freshly grated or
desiccated coconut

Put the minced pork and chopped prawns into a food processor and blend them to a smooth mousse. Transfer to a bowl. Put the garlic, shallots, ginger, salt, soy sauce and chilli oil in the food processor and blend to a smooth paste. Mix this thoroughly by hand into the pork-and-prawn mousse. Add the beaten egg white and stir it, in one direction only, with a fork or a wooden spoon for 2 minutes, until it gets difficult to stir.

Wet 2 dessertspoons with cold water and use them to form the mixture into egg-shaped dumplings (what the French call quenelles). Keep these on a plate lined with cling-film, taking care that none of them touch each other.

Bring half a panful of water to the boil, then add the lemon juice and ½ teaspoon of salt. Cook the dumplings in batches of 4–6 in the boiling water, for 6–8 minutes each batch. Scoop them out with a slotted spoon into a bowl. When all are cooked, set them aside while you make the sauce as described on page 162 and the rice.

To make the rice: if you are using fresh or frozen corn kernels, boil these first in water with a pinch of salt for 8–10 minutes. Canned sweetcorn need only be drained and rinsed. Whichever sort you use, break and mash the kernels lightly in a mortar or in a bowl with the back of a spoon.

Rinse the rice in several changes of water. Put it in a saucepan and pour in 600 ml / 1 pint water with ½ teaspoon of salt. Bring to the boil and simmer until almost all absorbed by the rice. Add the partly mashed sweetcorn and mix well. Transfer the mixture to a steamer or double saucepan. (If you are using desiccated coconut, stir this into the mixture now.) Steam for 15 minutes. Turn off the heat and leave to rest for 5 minutes. Then put the rice into a warm serving bowl. (If you are using fresh coconut, mix a large pinch of salt into it, and then stir the salted coconut into the sweetcorn rice just before serving.)

Reheat the sauce until it is just simmering. Put the cold dumplings into the sauce, adjust the seasoning and continue simmering for 4–5 minutes to reheat the dumplings. Add the pea shoots and leave them in the sauce for a few seconds only. Then transfer the dish to a deep serving platter and serve it immediately with the sweetcorn rice.

Indonesian spiced chicken rice

The chicken pieces for this dish are boiled with aromatic spices, then deep-fried, so that they remain tender under a deliciously crisp outer layer. The rice is cooked in the spiced stock. This dish is a favourite with everyone, especially children, who of course prefer to eat the chicken with their fingers.

for 4-6

2 tbsp groundnut oil
450 g / 1 lb basmati rice, soaked in cold water for 1 hour, then rinsed and drained
about 450 ml / ¾ pt vegetable oil, for deep-frying

for the stock
1 free-range organic chicken weighing about 1.5–1.8 kg / 3¼–4 lb, cut into 10 pieces
1 large red onion, finely chopped
2 tsp ground coriander
1 tsp ground cumin
a small stick of cinnamon
a pinch of freshly grated nutmeg
2 cloves
1 lemon grass stalk, bruised
1 tsp salt

to garnish
1 tbsp Crisp-fried Shallots (page 170)
a handful of flat-leaf parsley
2 tsp chopped chives
cucumber slices

Put all the ingredients for the stock in a large saucepan with 1.2 litres / 2 pints water, bring to the boil and cook until the chicken is cooked through, 45–60 minutes. Take the chicken pieces out and spread them on a tray lined with kitchen paper. They must be completely dry before they are deep-fried, so that the skin becomes crisp.

Put the groundnut oil into a large saucepan which has a tight-fitting lid. Heat the oil, then add the rice and stir it for 2 minutes. Add about 600 ml / 1 pint of the stock; if there is not quite enough stock, add some water. Bring to the boil and let the rice cook in the stock, uncovered, for about 10–15 minutes, until all the liquid has been absorbed by the rice. Add a little salt and stir the rice well with a wooden spoon. Put the lid on the pan tightly, lower the heat, and let the rice cook for 10–12 minutes more. Then, with the lid still tight, put the pan into a container that has 2–3 cm / about 1 inch of cold water in the bottom, and leave it there for 5 minutes. This will ensure that the crisp bottom layer of rice will separate from the pan and not stick to it.

While the rice is cooking, start frying the chicken pieces, in 2 batches, in hot oil in a wok or deep-fryer (see page 63). The whole frying time will be 20–25 minutes per batch; during this time, turn the chicken pieces over several times. Scoop the crisp golden chicken pieces out of the oil as soon as they're done, and set them to drain on kitchen paper.

Transfer the rice from its saucepan to a serving dish. Pile the fried chicken on top, with the crisp bits of rice from the bottom of the pan broken up and scattered over all. Arrange the garnishes on top of the chicken and serve straight away, asking everyone to help themselves.

nasi goreng

This is Indonesian fried rice. Its name means, precisely, 'fried rice' and is so well known that many people think fried rice dishes from other Southeast Asian countries must be 'nasi goreng' too. In fact anyone who has been to, say, Thailand and Indonesia will immediately recognize the versions there as quite different. Being Indonesian myself, I automatically believe people who tell me nasi goreng *is the best. This particular recipe is the plainest of all, which means that you can freeze and reheat it in a wok or a microwave oven after defrosting. It is good for serving hot, accompanied by any roast meat or grilled meat or fish, and with a side dish of plain boiled vegetables or a mixed salad. You can use basmati, Thai fragrant or any other long-grained rice.*

for 6-8

450 g / 1 lb rice (see introduction)
2 tbsp groundnut or corn oil
3 shallots, thinly sliced
2 garlic cloves, finely chopped
1–2 large red chilli(es),
deseeded and finely chopped
1 tsp finely chopped ginger root
1 tsp ground coriander
1 tsp paprika
2 small carrots, diced
3 cabbage leaves, finely shredded
225 g / 8 oz brown mushrooms, halved
2 tbsp tomato purée
2 tbsp light soy sauce
salt and pepper

to garnish
Crisp-fried Shallots (page 170)
roughly chopped flat-leaf parsley

At least 2 hours before frying, rinse the rice in 2 changes of cold water and then cook in a rice cooker or by the absorption method (see page 144).

When ready to cook, heat the oil in a wok and stir-fry the shallots, garlic, chillies and ginger for 1–2 minutes. Add the ground coriander, paprika and carrots, and stir-fry for 2 minutes more. Stir in the cabbage, mushrooms, tomato purée and soy sauce. Cover for a few minutes until the vegetables are cooked. Stir in salt and pepper, followed by the cold rice. Stir the rice around on a low heat, until all of it is well coated with the mixture of the vegetables and is getting hot. Adjust the seasoning with more soy sauce and salt if necessary.

Transfer to a serving platter and strew with the garnishes. Let everybody help themselves.

Notes: Newly cooked fried rice can be heated further in a microwave oven on full power for 2 minutes. If you want to freeze fried rice, wait until it is cold and then pack it in individual containers. Seal the containers well before storing them in the freezer. They can be frozen for up to 3 months. Defrost completely before heating the fried rice, then serve immediately.

crisp rice cakes with spiced minced duck

As an appetizer eaten with the fingers, crisp rice cakes are now to be found on the menus of modern Thai and Cambodian restaurants that serve eclectic or fusion food. Another important ingredient here is roasted rice which has been ground to a coarse powder. To make it, simply heat uncooked rice in a dry frying pan, stirring it continuously with a wooden spoon for about 4 minutes, so that every grain is nicely browned. It can be ground by hand in a mortar, or in a blender or a coffee-grinder; but don't grind it too fine.

for 6-8 as a first course

3–4 cups freshly cooked Thai fragrant rice
4 tbsp raw Thai fragrant rice
3 shallots, finely chopped
2–4 small chillies, chopped
2 tbsp groundnut oil,
plus more for deep-frying
6 skinless duck breast fillets, minced
6-cm / 2½-in piece of lemon grass stalk,
soft inner part only, finely chopped
4 tablespoons chicken stock
3 tbsp lemon juice
2 tbsp fish sauce
2 kaffir lime leaves, thinly sliced
salt
2 tbsp finely chopped spring onions
12–24 coriander leaves, for garnish

Well ahead, make the rice cakes: preheat the oven to 75°C / 165°F (lowest possible gas setting) and put the cooked rice on a baking tray. Roll or press into a layer about 1 cm / ½ inch thick. Put in the oven for at least 6 hours, preferably overnight. This removes every trace of moisture and the 'cake' will be brittle. Break it into biscuit-sized pieces and store in an airtight container.

Roast the raw Thai fragrant rice in a dry frying pan until lightly browned, then coarsely grind as described above.

Stir-fry the shallots and chillies in the oil for 1–2 minutes. Add the duck and stir-fry for 2 minutes more. Add the lemon grass, stock, lemon juice, fish sauce and lime leaves. Increase the heat and cook on a high heat until all the liquid is gone. Stir and adjust the seasoning (remember that fish sauce is very salty). Add the ground rice and spring onions, and stir for 2 more minutes.

Deep-fry the rice cakes (see page 63), 2 or 3 at a time, for about 2 minutes, or until the rice is puffed up and crisp. Serve the minced duck mixture on the rice cakes, garnished with the coriander leaves.

black rice paella

This is another recipe from a restaurant, this time in New York City, where Romy Dorotan and his wife, Amy, own and run a Filipino restaurant called Cendrillon. They are a very enterprising couple who often invite food writers, and chefs too, to cook during Amy's Asian cuisine promotions, and I was honoured when they invited me. Filipino cuisine, not surprisingly, has been much influenced by Spanish, but this paella is Romy's creation, using black glutinous rice and various seafood. If you order this at Cendrillon it will come to table in a clay pot, piping hot, and on top of the rice and buried inside it you'll find crab on the shell, large prawns, mussels, clams, scallops and sometimes lobster as well. Here I am giving you a simpler version that you can make at home, but still capturing the aroma and the taste of the sea!

for 4-6 or as a main course or 8-12 as a first course

450 g / 1 lb black rice
1 small onion, finely chopped
1 carrot, diced
4 tbsp olive oil
2 pandan leaves (optional)
1 tsp salt
1 tbsp chopped soft inner parts of a lemon grass stalk
3 garlic cloves, finely chopped
3 shallots, finely chopped
1 tsp finely chopped ginger
2 green chillies, deseeded and chopped
2 leeks, sliced
125 g / 4 oz fresh shiitake mushrooms, sliced
2 plum tomatoes, skinned and roughly chopped
2 slender aubergines, cubed
6 yard-long beans, cut into 2 cm / ¾ in lengths
450 g / 1 lb large raw prawns in the shell and with heads
1 cooked crab, cleaned and cut into quarters (optional)
6 clams
225 ml / 8 fl oz coconut milk
2 tbsp fish sauce (nam pla)
juice of ½ lemon
8 large scallops, each cut across into 2 discs

Rinse the rice in 2 changes of water, then drain. Sauté the onion and carrot in half the oil in a large pot over a moderate heat. Stir in the rice, add 850 ml / 1½ pints of water and bring to the boil. Add the pandan leaves, if using, and the salt. Reduce the heat to low and cover the pan. Simmer for about 20 minutes, or until the water has been absorbed and the rice is almost cooked. Transfer the rice to a large clay pot or casserole and set aside.

In another pan or wok, heat the remaining oil and add the lemon grass, garlic, shallots, ginger, chillies, leeks, mushrooms, tomatoes, aubergines and beans. Stir them around for 2 minutes or so over a moderate heat. Now add the prawns, crab if using, the clams and the coconut milk, and stir well. Season to taste with fish sauce and lemon juice.

Transfer this seafood mixture to the rice in the clay pot or casserole, and place the pot over a moderate heat. Simmer for 5–10 minutes, until the clams open, adding the scallops about halfway through. Serve immediately.

pan-seared bonito on green lentils

Here the tuna is 'twice-cooked' in order to infuse it with the flavours that it is to carry to the table. The first time, it is 'cooked' without fire but with vinegar and spices; the second time it is seared to lightly char it and warm it ready for serving on its bed of lentils. In this way you will avoid leaving it raw on the inside, but you will not be in danger of overcooking it.

for 4 as a one-dish meal

4 tuna steaks, each about 175 g / 6 oz
175–225 g / 6–8 oz green lentils
½ tsp salt
2 tbsp groundnut or sunflower oil
4 shallots, thinly sliced
2 garlic cloves, finely chopped
2 tsp finely chopped ginger root
2 tsp ground coriander
1 tsp ground cumin
½ tsp cayenne pepper
1 tsp salt
4–6 ripe tomatoes, skinned, deseeded and chopped
2 tbsp finely chopped parsley or fried sprigs, to garnish

for the marinade

2 tbsp lime juice
2 tsp rice vinegar
1 tsp salt
a pinch of cayenne pepper
1 tsp ground coriander

Make the marinade by mixing all the ingredients in a bowl and marinate the tuna steaks in it for about 30 minutes.

Rinse the lentils in 2 changes of water, then drain them. Put them in a pan with 1.6 litres / 3 pints of water. Bring to the boil and cook the lentils, keeping the water just bubbling, for 15 minutes. Add ½ teaspoon of salt and continue boiling for another 5 minutes. Drain.

Heat the oil in a wok or saucepan and stir-fry the shallots, garlic and ginger for 1–2 minutes. Add the spices and salt to taste, stir everything around and add the drained lentils. Cover the wok or pan for 2 minutes, then add the tomatoes, stir again and taste. Add more salt and cayenne pepper as required, and continue cooking for 2 minutes more. Set aside.

When ready to serve, heat the oil in a non-stick frying pan or rub it into a ridged griddle pan. When the pan is hot, place the tuna steaks on it side by side and sear them on each side for 1 minute, turning them over once. Cook them for 1 more minute, then turn off the heat.

Heat the lentils for about 3 minutes so that they are really hot. Divide them among 4 plates and place a tuna steak on top of each helping. Sprinkle chopped parsley over all and serve straight away.

braised beef with curried green lentils

The beef and the lentils are first cooked separately. This can be done well in advance.

for 6-8

3 tbsp groundnut or sunflower oil
1 kg / 2¼ lb silverside, cut into slices
8 tbsp Jungle Curry Paste (page 168)
300 ml / ½ pt thick coconut milk
salt and pepper
175–225 g / 6–8 oz green Puy lentils, rinsed and drained

Preheat the oven to 120ºC / 250ºF / Gas ½. Heat the oil in a heavy ovenproof pan. Brown the beef slices, turning several times, for 8–10 minutes. Add half the curry paste and turn again so all are coated. Add two-thirds of the coconut milk and simmer for 10 minutes. Season, cover and put in the oven for 60–90 minutes.

About half an hour before you want to serve, put the lentils in 225 ml / 8 fl oz cold water in a saucepan. Bring to the boil and boil for about 10 minutes. Drain.

Put the remaining curry paste and coconut milk in another pan. Bring to the boil and add the lentils. Cook on medium heat, stirring often, for 8 minutes or until the sauce is thick. Taste and add salt if necessary.

Put the lentils in a casserole, arrange the beef on top and pour the sauce over.

some basic recipes

As well as useful basic stocks, in this section you will find some of the most popular yet classic sauces, dips and curry pastes of tropical Asia. They are used in many of the recipes in this book or suggested as accompaniments. They are all made according to the principles of my 'new way', applying common sense, using ingredients available almost everywhere, but making no compromise on quality. All use fresh ingredients, but most can be stored in airtight containers for at least a few days. Some can be kept for much longer, if they are suitable for freezing in ice-cube trays. These will give you 'instant' flavours and enable to make your own 'convenience' food at short notice, and you will still have the real taste of Southeast Asia. Things like the sambals and relishes are also a good way of allowing you to add extra heat at the table for those whose taste buds are more used to hot flavours.

Thai piquant dressing

I use this dressing not only for salads but for many other dishes in this book. The quantity given below is sufficient to dress a generous bowl of salad for 4 to 6 people. I have prescribed the smallest number of chillies that will prevent the dressing being too mild, and the largest number beyond which it will become too fierce.

*The flavour of **palm sugar** makes a real difference in dressings such as this. It may be found in Oriental shops or even in supermarkets. It is procured by tapping the male flowers of certain palm trees, particularly the sugar-palm,* Arenga pinnata, *and then boiling it down to syrup, which is poured into moulds to set. As a result, the sugar comes to market in small round cakes, extremely hard but brittle. Before use, a cake must be broken up, with a cleaver or a heavy rolling-pin. The shards can be grated or dissolved in warm water. Palm sugar is often called by an adapted Indian name, jaggery.*

serves 4-6

1 tbsp grated palm sugar
or demerara sugar
3 tbsp warm water
1–4 fresh bird's-eye chillies,
deseeded and chopped
1 garlic clove, crushed
4 tbsp fish sauce (nam pla)
juice of 3 limes (about 4 tbsp)
3 tbsp chopped coriander leaves
2 tsp finely chopped lemon grass
(the soft inner part only)

In a bowl, dissolve the sugar in the warm water and add the rest of the ingredients. Mix well, and refrigerate until needed. The dressing will keep in the fridge for up to 48 hours.

piquant Vietnamese dip

To be authentic, if that's what you want to be, use nuoc mam, *the Vietnamese version of fish sauce. However,* nam pla, *which is what the Thais prefer, is exported all over the world and may be easier to find. As with the Thai Piquant Dressing above, I propose the use of this dip with many dishes in this book, not just with those that actually come from Vietnam.*

serves 4-6

about 4 tbsp lemon juice
or mild rice vinegar
about 1 tbsp caster sugar
1–4 bird's-eye chillies,
deseeded and chopped
4 tbsp fish sauce (see above)
2 spring onions, sliced into thin rounds
1 carrot, peeled and finely grated
2 tbsp chopped coriander or mint leaves,
or equal amounts of both

Put the lemon juice or vinegar in a glass bowl with the sugar. Stir to dissolve the sugar, then add all the other ingredients and mix them well with a spoon. Add more sugar and lemon juice to taste. Refrigerate until needed. This dip can be stored in the fridge for up to 48 hours.

peanut sauce *I have adapted this from various recipes widely known in Southeast Asia to make a basic peanut sauce that will go well as a dressing for vegetables, or as a dip and a sauce with grilled meat, fish or shellfish. This doesn't mean it has become bland – it is still an assertive, piquant sauce, full of Eastern flavour.*

makes about 300 ml / ½ pint

115 ml / 4 fl oz groundnut
or sunflower oil
225 g / 8 oz raw shelled (but still
with their pink skins) peanuts

for the spice paste
3 shallots or 1 onion, chopped
3 garlic cloves, chopped
1 tsp shrimp paste (page 122, optional)
½ tsp chilli powder
1 tsp ground coriander
½ tsp ground cumin
½ tsp sugar
1 tbsp dark soy sauce
½ tsp salt
2 tbsp tamarind water (page 164)
or lemon juice
2 tbsp olive oil

Heat the oil in a wok or saucepan and fry the peanuts for 4 minutes, stirring them frequently. With a slotted spoon, transfer them to a colander lined with absorbent paper and leave them to cool. Then grind them to a fine powder in a blender or coffee grinder.

Make the spice paste: put all the ingredients into a blender and blend until smooth. Transfer to a wok or large shallow saucepan and heat, stirring frequently, for 3–4 minutes.

Add 600 ml / 1 pt water and bring the sauce to the boil. Add the ground peanuts, stir, cover the wok or pan and simmer for 3 minutes. Uncover and continue to simmer, stirring often, for another 2 minutes, or until the sauce has reduced to the thickness required by the recipe. Adjust the seasoning if necessary.

This sauce can be stored for up to 1 week in an airtight jar in the fridge. It can also be frozen for up to 3 months. Thaw it out completely before reheating it in a saucepan. If it has become too thick, add a little water and continue heating until it reaches the right consistency for the recipe in which it is to be used.

soy sauce with chillies *I use this as a dipping sauce. It can also be used instead of salt to season any stir-fried, fried rice or noodle dish.*

***Soy sauce** hardly needs any introduction anywhere in today's world; to get so much flavour out of anything as bland as a soya bean seems to me almost miraculous. One of the natural components of properly-fermented soy sauce is monosodium glutamate, MSG - in very small quantities, too little to have any bad effect except on someone hyperallergic to it. Soy sauces come in many brands and qualities, but are generally classified into dark (or thick) and light. All are salty, but dark soys tend to be less salty and some are downright sweet (especially those from Indonesia, labelled* kecap manis *– sweet ketjap). Kikkoman is an excellent general-purpose soy, and counts as dark (i.e. relatively mild); it is probably the best for a condiment, and is good for cooking.*

makes about 6 tablespoons

4 tbsp light or dark soy sauce
2–6 bird's-eye chillies,
deseeded (or not) and finely chopped
1 shallot, finely chopped
1 tbsp lime or lemon juice
1 tsp sugar (if light soy sauce is used)

Mix all the ingredients together in a small bowl and use as needed. This will keep in the fridge for up to a week.

coconut sambal

*When buying a **coconut**, hold it close to your ear and give it a shake. You should hear a faint sloshing sound that indicates there is some liquid inside. If you don't, the nut is probably a bit too old. To open a coconut: first, hold it loosely in one hand and give the shell repeated hard taps with a hammer or the back of a cleaver. Keep turning the nut so that the tapping loosens the flesh and separates it as much as possible from the shell. Put the nut in a plastic bag, rest it on a firm surface, and give one or two heavy blows with the hammer or cleaver. The shell will split, and probably so will the layer of flesh inside, releasing any water that is there. You can strain this and drink it but it's hardly worth it. Break the firm white layer of flesh into pieces. If you need pure white flesh for cooking (or ice-cream), peel off the brown outer layer; otherwise, don't bother. See page 179 for making coconut milk.*

makes about 200 g / 7 oz

115–170 g / 4–6 oz grated, desiccated, or frozen grated coconut

for the spice paste
2 shallots, chopped
2 garlic cloves, chopped
2–6 large red chillies, deseeded and chopped
2 red bird's-eye chillies, chopped (optional)
2 tsp chopped ginger
2 kaffir lime leaves, shredded
2 tbsp tamarind water (page 164) or lime juice
2 tbsp vegetable oil
1 tsp salt

First make the spice paste: put all the ingredients into a blender and blend until smooth. Transfer to a saucepan and cook on a medium heat, stirring from time to time, for 6–8 minutes.

Stir in the coconut, with 115 ml / 4 fl oz cold water if using desiccated coconut, and continue cooking, stirring more often now, until all the liquid has been absorbed but the sambal is still quite moist. Taste and add more salt if needed.

Serve at room temperature as a relish, dressing, or garnish, as suggested in the recipe for the dish it is to accompany. This sambal will stay fresh in the fridge for up to 48 hours.

balachaung (dried prawn sambal)

This is a Burmese hot relish, made of dried prawns or shrimps with plenty of garlic and chillies. It can be kept in an airtight jar in the fridge for a month. It is worth making a good quantity.

makes about 300 g / 10½ oz

225 g / 8 oz dried shrimps
3 tbsp vegetable oil
4 shallots, finely chopped
4 garlic cloves, thinly sliced
2 tsp sesame oil
2–4 red chillies, deseeded and finely chopped, or ½–1 teaspoon chilli powder
2 tsp finely chopped ginger
½ tsp ground turmeric
2 tbsp hot water
juice of 1 lime or lemon
½ tsp salt, or more to taste

Soak the dried shrimps in hot water for 10 minutes, drain and chop with a sharp knife, or put them in a small blender and blend until fine. Set aside.

Heat the oil in a wok or saucepan, and fry the shallots and garlic until lightly coloured. Take out with a slotted spoon and reserve.

Add the sesame oil to the wok or pan, heat and add the rest of the ingredients, except the hot water, the lime or lemon juice and the salt. Fry, stirring all the time, for 2 minutes. Add the ground shrimps and continue stir-frying for another minute. Now, add the water and lime or lemon juice. Stir again until the liquid is absorbed by the shrimps.

The balachaung is now ready. For the right texture, the mixture should remain moist, not be dry; if it seems too dry, add a little more hot water or citrus juice. Taste and adjust the seasoning with salt and more citrus juice if necessary.

sambal goreng sauce

Sambal goreng *is a generic term for a great number of everyday dishes in Indonesia and Malaysia. Don't confuse it with the word* sambal, *which is a relish made with lots of chillies.* Sambal goreng *sauce can be made at any time and can be eaten with any staple – rice, potatoes, noodles or pasta.*

makes about 450 ml / ¾ pint

4 tbsp hot water
1 can (400 ml / 14 fl oz) of coconut milk
2–3 tomatoes, skinned, deseeded, and roughly chopped

for the spice paste
4 shallots, chopped
2 garlic cloves, chopped
1 tsp chopped ginger
2–6 large red chillies, deseeded and chopped
2 candlenuts or macadamia nuts, or 4 blanched almonds, chopped
1 tsp roasted shrimp paste (balachan, see page 160, optional)
2 tsp roasted coriander seeds, crushed
1 tsp paprika
1 tsp salt
2 tbsp tamarind water (page 164)
2 tbsp groundnut oil or sunflower oil

First make the spice paste: put all the ingredients in a blender with 2 tablespoons cold water and blend until smooth. Transfer to a saucepan, bring to the boil and cook, stirring often, for 6–8 minutes.

Add the hot water and continue cooking for 5 minutes. Add the coconut milk and simmer, stirring occasionally, for about 15 minutes, to let the sauce reduce a little. Taste and adjust the seasoning with more salt and tamarind water if necessary, then add the tomatoes and continue cooking for 2 minutes more.

The sauce is now ready to be served immediately, or to be left to cool and stored in an airtight jar in the fridge for up to 3 days. If you chill it, reheat on a low heat for about 4–6 minutes before serving.

fresh tomato sambal

I use this sambal *for the Maluku Fish Cakes and Spiced Prawns on page 32. That part of eastern Indonesia – the Moluccas, as Europeans used to call the islands – and North Sulawesi still retain a lot of Portuguese influence in their cooking. Whether the local people know that tomatoes, chilli peppers and potatoes all reached here from South America I can't say, but the Indonesian word* 'sambal' *can be correctly translated as 'salsa'.*

makes about 300 ml / ½ pint

2–4 fresh bird's-eye chillies
4–6 plum or vine tomatoes
2 shallots, very thinly sliced
2 tbsp white distilled vinegar
2 tsp caster sugar
1 tsp chopped mint or coriander leaves
½–1 tsp salt

Deseed and chop the chillies. Skin, deseed and dice the tomatoes small. In a glass bowl, mix all the ingredients except the tomatoes, stirring them with a spoon until the sugar and salt are dissolved. Taste and add more salt if needed.

Lastly add the diced tomatoes. Mix well and serve at room temperature.

red pepper and tomato sauce

This is the latest development in my experimenting with this sauce. By pre-roasting the peppers and tomatoes in the oven, you will give the sauce a more subtle and delicious flavour. The alternative is to char the skins of the peppers and tomatoes under the grill or over a charcoal fire.

makes about 300 ml / ½ pint

3 red peppers
6 tomatoes
3 tbsp vegetable oil
4 shallots, thinly sliced
2 garlic cloves, thinly sliced
1 tsp chopped ginger
2 tbsp finely chopped flat-leaf parsley
½–1 tsp salt
1 tbsp soy sauce
½–1 tsp brown sugar

Preheat the oven to 180ºC / 350ºF / Gas 4 and roast the peppers and tomatoes on a baking tray for 25 minutes.

Remove and, when cool enough to handle, peel them and deseed them over a sieve above a bowl so as to catch the juices. Chop the flesh and keep it aside in another bowl.

Heat the oil in a medium saucepan, add the shallots, garlic and ginger, and stir-fry for 2–3 minutes.

Add the rest of the ingredients, including the reserved cooking juices, the chopped peppers and tomatoes, together with 4 tablespoons of water. Simmer for 10 minutes. Taste and add salt if necessary.

Serve the sauce, just as it is, hot or warm, in a bowl. Alternatively, blend the sauce in a blender, heat it again for a minute or so and serve it hot. To make it smoother still, you can pour it from the blender through a sieve. In that case, adjust the seasoning again before serving.

mild curry sauce

This sauce goes well with many dishes described in this book, but it is particularly suitable for the Pepper-crusted Fillet Steak on page 104. If you want it stronger and spicier, double the quantities of ground coriander, cumin and chilli.

makes just under 600 ml / 1 pint

4 shallots or 1 large onion, finely chopped
3 garlic cloves, chopped
1 tsp chopped ginger
3 tbsp olive oil or groundnut oil
½ tsp chilli powder
2 tsp ground coriander
1 tsp ground cumin
½ tsp ground turmeric
2 tbsp ground almonds
700 ml / 1½ pints chicken stock or water
1 tsp salt, or more to taste
200 ml / 7 fl oz plain yoghurt
2 green cardamoms
1 bay leaf
2 cloves
2 tbsp chopped mint (optional)

In a blender or food processor (or using a pestle and mortar), blend the shallots or onion, garlic and ginger with the oil and 2 tablespoons of water until smooth.

Simmer this in a saucepan for 4–5 minutes, stirring often. Then add the chilli, coriander, cumin, turmeric and almonds, and stir for 2 minutes. Add the stock or water, a little at a time, continuing to stir for a minute or so. Season with salt and let the sauce simmer for 15 minutes.

Add the yoghurt, a spoonful at a time, stirring vigorously so that it does not curdle. (If it does curdle, put the whole lot into a liquidizer and run the machine for a few seconds before putting the sauce back in the pan.) Add the cardamoms, bay leaf and cloves. Simmer for another 3 minutes. Up to this point, the sauce can be made up to 24 hours in advance.

When you are ready to serve it, reheat the sauce gently, take out the cardamoms, bay leaf and cloves, adjust the seasoning and add the chopped mint if you wish.

southeast asian flavourings

These essential Asian flavours are all pungent, strong-tasting, complex and unlike anything that is familiar to most Western palates.

Fish sauce Fish sauces are really typical of Southeast Asia. With their pungency and saltiness, their function is to bring out the flavours of the dish without themselves being noticed. Therefore, they should be used sparingly. Of those available in London, most of which are from Thailand, my favourite is called Squid, though it is not made from squid. In these recipes I use the Thai name, *nam pla*, meaning 'fish sauce'. Occasionally, however, the Vietnamese *nuoc mam* is preferable. Either can be used to substitute for the other.

Dried anchovies ❷ These reach Chinese and other food shops in London and New York, usually in plastic packets labelled '*Ikan Bilis*' (*ikan* is fish). This tends to be used as a catch-all name for several species of small, silvery fish (which might equally well be called whitebait), caught in huge shoals off tropical coasts and dried and salted whole. In Malaysia they are often added to curries, but elsewhere they are deep-fried and used as a garnish.

Dried shrimp Tiny salted and dried shrimp (**❷**, bottom), sometimes labelled 'dried prawns', are sold in Asian stores and will keep for a long time. They are not meant to be reconstituted, but are used as a flavouring, although they are generally soaked in hot water for 5–10 minutes prior to use. See also Shrimp Paste, page 122.

Soy sauce, see page 159.

Chillies and chilli sauces As a rough guide, the smaller and thinner the chilli, the hotter it is, at least where Southeast Asian chillies are concerned. The smallest and hottest are the little bird's-eye chillies (**❸** top left), but any single chilli can turn out unexpectedly bland or boisterous when you bite into it. Red or green – the colour makes no difference. The active component is capsaicin, a chemical produced mainly in the seeds and placental tissue, which is why in most of the recipes in this book you are asked to deseed your chillies. I don't do this, of course, when I am cooking for Indonesian friends. The capsaicin does not actually burn your insides or cause any harm whatever, and chillies are full of vitamin C, so they actually do you good. However, wash your hands after handling chillies, and keep your fingers away from your eyes. If your mouth becomes unbearably hot while eating chillied food, the best coolant is plain boiled rice, preferably cold, or cucumber, or cold milk or yoghurt. Overheating is a common excuse for ordering more chilled beer, but this gives only temporary relief. Capsaicin is soluble in alcohol, but beer doesn't contain enough to be helpful.

Whole fresh chillies (**❸**) are easy to find – even supermarkets now sell them, though small Asian food stores usually charge much lower prices. Dried chillies (**❹**) are at least as hot as fresh, or hotter. Chilli powder and chilli flakes are useful if you use a lot of chilli, and ranges of sambals – chilli sauces, many of them with additional spices – are marketed in delicatessens by several companies, mostly in the Netherlands.

Tamarind, tamarind water Such a romantic-sounding name, so unromantic when you see it, either in the pod, (**❶** top), or in the shop. Tamarind is essential as a flavour in Asian food. You buy it, usually, as pulp, pressed into dark brown blocks, labelled 'tamarind paste' (**❶** bottom). The best way to use it is to make tamarind water.

Break a piece from the block and put in a pan with about 10 times its own weight in water. Heat gently – it doesn't need to boil – and knead the tamarind with your hand or a wooden spoon for 2–3 minutes so that it breaks up and releases its juices. You can, of course, vary the strength by using more or less pulp. Sieve the contents of the pan, discarding the solids. The water will transmit the aromatic sourness of tamarind to whatever you cook with it. It will keep in the fridge for a week.

red curry paste

This gets its name from making use of red chillies, but, surprisingly, is usually milder than the Green Curry Paste. Vegetarians can omit the shrimp paste and fish sauce. For instructions on freezing, see Green Curry Paste below.

makes about 450 ml / ¾ pint (enough for curry for 10-12)

3 tbsp roasted coriander seeds

2 tsp roasted cumin seeds

5–10 large red chillies, deseeded and chopped

5 shallots, chopped

3 garlic cloves, chopped

1 tbsp chopped galangal (page 109)

3 kaffir lime leaves, chopped

1 tbsp chopped lemon grass

2 tsp paprika

1 tsp salt

3 tbsp vegetable oil

2 tbsp tamarind water (page 164)

Put all the ingredients in a blender or food processor with 4 tablespoons water and blend until smooth.

Transfer to a saucepan and cook, stirring frequently, over a low heat for 4 minutes. Add 300 ml / ½ pint more water, bring to the boil, cover the pan and simmer for 30–45 minutes. The paste is now ready to be used as directed in the recipes.

If the paste is not all to be used at once, leave it to get cold before storing it in a jar in the fridge or in the ice-cube tray in the freezer.

green curry paste

This very popular, pungent curry paste gets its name from its use of lots of green chillies and coriander leaves. The amount given here is adequate for a curry for 10–12 people as a main course. Use 4 tablespoonfuls of paste for 4 people. Freeze the unused paste by putting 1 tablespoonful into each compartment of an ice-cube tray. Freeze for at least 24 hours, then take the cubes from the tray and store them in a freezer bag. Use within 3 months. Vegetarians omit the shrimp paste.

3 tbsp coriander seeds

2 tsp cumin seeds

2–4 green chillies, deseeded (or not if you prefer) and chopped

2 green peppers, deseeded and chopped

6 shallots, chopped

3 garlic cloves, chopped

1 tsp shrimp paste

4 tbsp chopped coriander leaves, plus 2 tsp chopped roots (optional)

2 tsp chopped lemon grass

½ in piece of fresh galangal, finely chopped, or 1 tsp ground

4 tbsp tamarind water (see page 164)

2 tbsp groundnut or vegetable oil

1 tsp salt

Roast the coriander and cumin seeds in a dry frying pan over moderate heat, stirring frequently, until they just start to brown. Be careful not to burn them or they will taste bitter.

Put these and all the other ingredients in a blender or food processor with 2–3 spoonfuls of water and process for about 2 minutes until you have a smooth, free-flowing paste.

Transfer this to a saucepan, heat and simmer for 5–8 minutes, stirring occasionally. Add 1¼ cups of cold water and bring it back to the boil. Cover the pan, then simmer for 30–45 minutes.

The paste is now ready to use as directed by the recipe, or to be frozen as described above.

jungle curry paste

I learned about the different kinds of curry paste when I attended the Thai Cooking School at the Oriental Hotel in Bangkok about ten years ago. The Thais classify their curries under two main headings: 'city' and 'jungle'. The conclusion that I drew for myself was that jungle curry paste, whether red, green or yellow, should be stronger than that for city curry. On my most recent visit to Thailand, I stopped at the Regent Resort in Chiang Mai and ate a really spicy and chilli-hot curry of spare ribs. The menu simply said 'Hung Lay Curry', and this is indeed a traditional northern Thai dish, with its origins in Burma, not very far away. No coconut milk is used for this curry (a distinguishing feature of jungle curries), and my further conclusion is now that jungle curry and hung lay use the same paste. You can make it either red or green (as in the Jungle Curry on page 112) just by choosing red or green chillies. In Thailand, pork spare ribs are a good choice of meat to use with it. I myself prefer to use shank of lamb or short ribs of beef.

makes about 300 ml / ½ pint

2–6 green or red bird's-eye chillies, chopped
1 green or red pepper, deseeded and chopped
6 shallots, chopped
4 garlic cloves, chopped
2 tsp chopped lemon grass
2 tsp chopped galangal
2 tsp chopped coriander root
1 tsp kaffir lime zest or 2 kaffir lime leaves, shredded
1 tsp roasted shrimp paste (page 122)
½ tsp salt
1 tsp whole black pepper
2 tsp fish sauce (nam pla)
2 tbsp tamarind water (page 164)
2 tbsp groundnut oil

Blend all the ingredients until smooth.

Transfer the paste to a saucepan, bring to the boil and simmer, stirring often, for 4–6 minutes. The paste is now ready to use.

laksa paste

Laksa paste, like the curry pastes, can be made well in advance and stored in the fridge for up to 7 days. It can be frozen in an ice-cube tray or small self-sealing plastic freezer bags. It's a good idea to label these clearly and indelibly, and to write the date on them – especially if you are storing a collection of pastes in your freezer. More or less a variation on the Sambal Goreng earlier, laksa paste is usually used for laksa soupy stews and other seafood dishes.

makes about 300 ml / ½ pint

4–6 large red chillies, deseeded and chopped
6 shallots, chopped
3 garlic cloves, chopped
6 candlenuts or 10 blanched almonds, chopped
2 tsp chopped ginger
2 tsp chopped galangal (page 109)
2 tbsp coriander seeds, roughly crushed
½ tsp shrimp paste (optional)
1 tsp salt
3 tbsp tamarind water (page 164)
2 tbsp groundnut or vegetable oil

Put all the ingredients in a blender or food processor and process for 1 minute, then add 175 ml / 6 fl oz water and continue processing for 2 more minutes.

Transfer the smooth paste to a saucepan and cook at just above simmering point for 40 minutes.

Leave the paste to get cold and store as described above. Use as required, in the quantities given in the recipes.

rujak sauce

This piquant sauce is very popular in Indonesia and Malaysia. People in those countries use it mainly to dress salads of sour fruit. Recently, however, many Oriental chefs have begun to use it as a sauce for steaks and other grilled meats. Here I recommend it as a spicy dipping sauce.

for 4 (makes 115 ml / 4 fl oz)

4 tbsp hot water
60 g / 2 oz grated palm sugar (page 158) or soft brown sugar
½ tsp grilled shrimp paste (page 122)
2 tbsp juice of fresh limes or tamarind water (page 164)
1 tsp salt
2–4 bird's-eye chillies, finely chopped
4 spring onions, thinly sliced (optional)

Mix everything except the spring onions, if using, in a glass bowl, stirring to dissolve the sugar, shrimp paste and salt.

Divide among several small bowls so each person has their own, and scatter over the sliced spring onion, if using.

crisp-fried ginger
This is a good way of preserving ginger that also allows it to be used as an ingredient in savoury dishes. However, I include it primarily as a garnish for several of the dishes in this book.

makes 225 g / 8 oz

450 g / 1 lb ginger, thinly peeled
vegetable oil, for deep-frying

With a sharp knife, slice the ginger very thinly at an angle. Pile these thin slices on top of each other, a few at a time, and cut into very tiny matchsticks.

Blanch the ginger in boiling water for 30 seconds. Refresh in cold water, drain and pat dry with kitchen paper.

Heat about 115 ml / 4 fl oz of oil in a small pan or wok. Deep-fry the ginger, stirring all the time, for about 2 minutes or until crisp. Drain on kitchen paper.

Keep in an airtight container until needed. Any leftovers after using them as a garnish can be used in any dish that specifies chopped ginger.

crisp-fried shallots
Nowadays, I think, crisp fried onions can be bought ready-made in most supermarkets anywhere in the world, and they are very good as long as you don't keep them beyond their best-by dates. If you want to make your own, use shallots rather than onions. Shallots fry crisp without being coated in flour.

makes about 225 g / 8 oz

150 ml / ¼ pint vegetable oil
450 g / 1 lb shallots, thinly sliced

Heat the oil in a wok or non-stick frying pan until a slice of shallot dropped into it sizzles immediately. Fry the shallots in 2 batches, stirring all the time, for 3–4 minutes each batch, or until crisp and golden brown. Take out of the pan with a slotted spoon, drain in a colander and let cool. In an airtight container, they will stay fresh and crisp for up to a week – there's no need to refrigerate.

dried anchovy relish
These make an excellent dry relish or garnish, and are also a popular salty, crunchy snack with drinks. They must be fried very crisp, and served and eaten before they become in the least stale or soft. In an airtight container, they should stay in peak condition for at least 4 days. Do not refrigerate! Look for the anchovies without heads that are sold in Oriental food stores, labelled ikan teri *or* ikan bilis. *If you can only get them with heads still on, cut these off and discard.*

makes about 350 g / 12 oz

225 ml / 8 fl oz (or more)
groundnut or corn oil
450 g / 1 lb dried anchovies

Heat the oil in a wok to 180°C / 350°F and deep-fry the anchovies in 2 batches for 3 minutes each batch, stirring often. With a slotted spoon, transfer them to a tray lined with kitchen paper to drain.

For real crispness, you need to fry them a second time, for 1–2 minutes. Take care they do not start to burn. Drain on kitchen paper as before. Leave to cool and then store in an airtight container.

cucumber and coriander leaf relish *This is a*

basic cucumber relish that can be combined with other herbs if you don't like coriander,
or if none is available. Alternatives could be parsley – curly or flat-leaf – basil, mint,
chives or even spring onions.

serves 4-6

1 cucumber, peeled or unpeeled,
cut in half lengthwise
6 tbsp rice or cider vinegar
6 tbsp warm water
2 tsp caster sugar
1 tsp salt
1–4 bird's-eye chillies,
deseeded and finely chopped
2 shallots, thinly sliced
a large handful of coriander leaves
or other herbs (see above), roughly
chopped or shredded

Scrape out and discard the seeds from the cucumber, then slice it into thin half-moons.

Put the vinegar and water in a glass bowl, add the sugar and salt, and stir to dissolve them. Then add all the other ingredients, including the cucumber slices and the herb of your choice. Leave it all to stand for at least 10–15 minutes, then serve at room temperature.

onion and tamarind chutney *When I make this chutney,*

what I am aiming for are a texture and consistency just firm enough to let me spread it
on slices of cucumber, or a piece of bread or toast, but at the same time soft enough
for the chutney to be served as a dipping sauce. The apples help to provide this texture,
and of course they give an extra dimension of flavour.

makes about 1.5 kg / 3 lb

115 ml / 4 fl oz rice vinegar
or cider vinegar
675 g / 1½ lb red onions, chopped
450 g / 1 lb apples (Granny Smith
or Cox's), peeled, cored and chopped
300 ml / ½ pint thick tamarind
water (see page 164)
5 garlic cloves, chopped
2 large red chillies, deseeded
and finely chopped
150 g / 5 oz dark soft sugar
or grated palm sugar
2 tsp finely chopped ginger
½ tsp freshly grated nutmeg
1 tbsp salt

Put the vinegar, onions, apples, tamarind water, garlic and chillies in a non-reactive saucepan (stainless steel or enamelled). Bring the liquid to the boil, and cook on a medium heat for 30–40 minutes, stirring occasionally to make sure the mixture doesn't burn.

Add the rest of the ingredients and continue cooking for another 10 minutes over a low heat. Taste and adjust the seasoning by adding more salt and/or sugar as required.

This chutney can be eaten straight away, at room temperature, or stored in sterilized airtight jars. It has a shelf life of at least 3 months.

basic vegetable stock
You can choose whether to make a simple vegetable stock or one that has some Southeast Asian ingredients – kaffir lime leaf, ginger, lemon grass and galangal.

makes 1.7-2.3 litres / 3-4 pints

2 medium carrots, each cut into 4 pieces
1 onion, quartered
1 tsp salt

for the Southeast Asian ingredients (optional)
2 kaffir lime leaves
2 cm / ¾ in piece of ginger
1 lemon grass stalk, cut across into 3
2 cm / ¾ in piece of galangal (page 109)

For a basic vegetable stock: bring 2.3 litres / 4 pints cold water to the boil and add the carrots, onion and salt. Simmer, skimming often, for 40–45 minutes. Strain the stock into a bowl and refrigerate until needed.

To incorporate the optional Southeast Asian ingredients, add them about 10 minutes before the end of cooking and strain as above.

Either way, the stock can be kept for up to 3 days in the fridge, or frozen for up to 3 months.

basic chicken stock
For a good chicken stock, you definitely need a whole chicken. Cut it into 16 pieces, chopping through the bones. This is a handy Oriental trick for making equal-sized portions. Using a sharp heavy knife or a cleaver, first cut the bird in half lengthwise, then cut off the thighs and drumsticks and the wings at the joints, then chop each thigh and drumstick across into two. Finally cut across each breast and carcass to divide them into three pieces, making 16 pieces in all. (Warning: it's not a problem when making stock, but by chopping the bones in this way, you will probably end up with some splinters. Make sure that everyone who eats chicken cut this way knows about these and takes care not to swallow any.) Wash the pieces well, taking special care to wash out every trace of the giblets from the carcass. Don't be tempted to add any part of the giblets to the stock, as it can make it bitter if the giblets haven't been well cleaned.

You can add some distinctive Southeast Asian flavouring as with the vegetable stock if you like, but chicken stock is usually made quite plain in the region to allow a wide range of ingredients to be added in the dishes in which it is used.

makes about 1.2 litres / 2 pints

1 chicken, cut up and cleaned as described above
1 tsp salt

Put the chicken pieces and salt into a large saucepan with 2.3–2.8 litres / 4–5 pints cold water. Bring to the boil and let boil for 5 minutes. Skim off all the froth that comes to the surface.

Reduce the heat and let the stock bubble gently for up to 2 hours, skimming from time to time and adding more water if a lot of it boils away.

Strain the stock through a sieve lined with muslin and refrigerate until needed (up to 3 days). The stock can also be frozen for up to 3 months.

dashi
This widely used Japanese fish stock is made from dried bonito tuna flakes (flaked dried tuna) and konbu (dried kelp).

makes 1-2 litres / 2-3 pints

a small piece of konbu
60 g / 2 oz bonito flakes

Put 1–2 litres / 2–3 pints of cold water into a saucepan add the konbu and bring the water almost, but not quite, to the boil. Remove and discard the konbu.

Now bring the water back to the boil and add the bonito flakes. Lower the heat and simmer for 4–5 minutes. Remove the pan from the heat, leave it covered for 5 minutes, then strain the stock through a sieve lined with muslin into a bowl.

Refrigerate until needed (up to 4 days).

quick fish stock
Use whatever large fish is to hand – I like to use most white fish, trout, salmon or turbot.

makes about 1.2 litres / 2 pints

well-cleaned head and bones
of 1 large fish
handful of prawn shells (optional)
60 g / 2 oz bonito flakes

Put 1–2 litres / 2–3 pints of cold water into a saucepan. Add the fish trimmings and prawn shells if using them. Bring to the boil and simmer for 5–6 minutes, skimming off the froth at short intervals. Strain this stock into another saucepan.

Bring the clear stock to the boil, add the bonito flakes and simmer for another 4–5 minutes. Remove from heat, cover the pan and leave undisturbed for 5 minutes.

Strain the stock into a bowl through a sieve lined with muslin. Refrigerate the stock until needed (it will keep for up to 4 days).

sweet dishes

It is not the custom in Southeast Asia to serve sweets such as those described here as puddings or desserts. Sweets are regarded simply as snacks, to be eaten when and where you feel the need for one. They do, however, have a social function as well: they are for serving to anyone who drops in or comes visiting. They are also for eating at any family gathering, formal or informal, and they are there, too, simply as a self-indulgence, when you are having a cup of coffee or tea. Obviously they can be eaten as dessert, but they are generally quite heavy so are best served after a fairly light meal. To follow anything more substantial, it's probably best to do as we would do in Southeast Asia and just have fruit or a fruit salad.

avocado ice-cream

Avocados grow prolifically in many parts of Southeast Asia, and we always regard them as fruit. A ripe avocado is usually served, not as a starter with French or some other piquant dressing, but as a dessert or snack, heavily sweetened with sugar and coconut milk or condensed milk, and often whipped up into a mousse. A natural progression is to freeze this and serve it as ice-cream, and it can taste very good. Here, I make my avocado ice-cream with coconut milk, which means that it is suitable for vegans. If you prefer to make it with double cream and cows' milk, it will be equally delicious.

for 4-6

600 ml / 1 pint thick coconut milk or canned coconut milk (see opposite) or 300 ml / ½ pint double cream mixed with 300 ml / ½ pint milk
4 small ripe avocados, each about 175 g / 6 oz
8 tbsp lemon or lime juice
10 level tbsp icing sugar

Gently heat the coconut milk or milk and cream mixture in the pan until it is at simmering point, then transfer it to a bowl to cool.

Halve the avocados, stone and peel them, chop the flesh and mix it with lemon or lime juice in a glass bowl. When the coconut milk is cold, pour it into a blender, then pour the avocado and the icing sugar on top of it. Blend until smooth and creamy.

Transfer this mix to a sorbetière or ice-cream maker and churn until the bits that cling to the side of the container are frozen. Scoop the ice-cream into a plastic container and put in the freezer. Keep frozen until required, remembering to transfer the ice-cream to the fridge 45 minutes before serving to allow it to 'ripen'.

black glutinous rice ice-cream

The basis of this is the Black Glutinous Rice Porridge on page 181. You can make the porridge into a sorbet by simply adding 2 tablespoonfuls of glucose to the mix and then churning it in a sorbetière. To make it into a deliciously creamy ice-cream is scarcely any more difficult.

for 6-8

Black rice porridge (page 181)
2 tbsp liquid glucose
600 ml / 1 pint double cream

Put the porridge, glucose and cream into a blender and blend until smooth.

Churn the mixture in a sorbetière or ice-cream maker until the bits that cling to the sides of the machine are frozen. Scoop the ice-cream into a plastic container and store in the freezer.

Keep frozen until required, but remember to transfer the ice-cream to the fridge 1 hour before serving.

fried bananas with grated coconut

Fried bananas are familiar just about everywhere. In tropical Asia, however, we have a particular type of banana that is exactly right for frying, but unfortunately it is not available everywhere. When I fry bananas at home in Wimbledon I use the ordinary supermarket ones, usually imported from the West Indies. A good alternative is to use ripe plantains, which are not hard to find. Asians usually eat fried bananas not for dessert but as a tea-time or morning-coffee snack. Freshly grated coconut is often served with them to give a contrasting texture. See page 160 for buying and preparing fresh coconuts.

*To make your own **coconut milk**, put the chopped flesh from a fresh coconut into your blender and heat about 600 ml / 1 pint of water until it is hot but not boiling. Add half of this water to the contents of the blender, and blend for 20–30 seconds. Pour the liquid through a fine sieve, and press out every drop you can. Then put the coconut solids back into the blender, pour on the other half of the hot water, and repeat the whole process. You will then have a pint jugful of averagely-thick coconut milk. If you are using desiccated coconut, you can get the same result by using about 350 g / 12 oz of it into the blender and following the same procedure. This will give the same quantity of milk, but it will be somewhat thicker.*

You can keep this coconut milk in the fridge for at most 48 hours. If the thicker 'cream' floats to the top, simply give it a stir (or skim it off and use it as coconut cream). Coconut milk cannot be frozen, and if you are cooking for the freezer the milk, which is usually added towards the end of cooking, should be omitted until the dish is thawed and reheated.

*If you can't get fresh coconut or haven't the time to make coconut milk, **creamed coconut** is sold in blocks (sometimes in the chilled counter), like a hard, white margarine. It is very useful for giving flavour and a little thickening in a number of dishes. It needs to be cut into small pieces – either by chopping with a sharp knife, or shaving thin slices off it. These usually go into the blender with other ingredients. Alternatively, they can be added to a sauce in the last few minutes of cooking to thicken it.*

for 4–6

4 medium-sized fairly ripe bananas,
or 2 ripe plantains
90 g / 3 oz rice flour
30 g / 1 oz melted butter
225 ml / 8 fl oz coconut milk (see above)
a pinch of salt
clarified butter, for frying
½ fresh coconut, white flesh only, grated

Peel the bananas or plantains and cut each one lengthwise down the middle, then cut each half across into 2 pieces if using bananas or 3 if using plantains. Alternatively, cut them into not-too-thin round slices.

Mix the flour, butter, coconut milk and salt into a smooth batter. Coat the banana or plantain pieces well with this batter, and fry in clarified butter until golden brown on both sides.

Scatter the grated coconut on top and serve hot or warm.

black glutinous rice porridge

This porridge, which is not really black but a lovely deep purple, is the basis of the delicious black rice sorbet I developed several years ago (the recipe is on page 178). The porridge, served hot or warm, will not fail to attract people, whether it is for breakfast or as a dessert. If you don't have any fruit, dress the porridge with its traditional accompaniment of thick coconut milk seasoned with salt, or just plenty of cream.

for 4-6

1.5 litres / 2¾ pints coconut milk
(or two 400 ml / 14 fl oz cans plus a
canful of water)
85 g / 3 oz black glutinous rice,
soaked in cold water for 2–8 hours,
then drained
½ tsp salt
1 small cinnamon stick
3 tbsp granulated sugar
mango slices, blackberries
and blueberries, to serve (optional)

Put the coconut milk in a saucepan with the rice, add the salt and cinnamon stick, and bring to the boil. Simmer slowly for 10 minutes, then add the sugar.

Continue to simmer, stirring often, until the porridge is thick, 60–70 minutes.

Serve the porridge hot or warm, topped with some fruit if you like.

tropical fruit salad

There are so many choices of fruit that the possibilities may seem endless and easy. In a sense this is so, but composing a salad of really satisfying harmonies and contrasts of taste and texture can benefit from a little guidance. From experience, I would never add sugar or sugar syrup, though this is customarily done in Asia, nor would I pour liqueur over a salad of fresh fruit. Here are all the lovely golden colours, and flavours, in one bowl.

for 6–8

1 large pineapple
2 ripe mangoes
5 large oranges
1 small golden watermelon
or Charentais melon
juice of 1 lemon or lime
6 passion fruit

Peel the pineapple, mangoes and 4 of the oranges. Take the eyes out of the pineapple and cut it in half lengthwise. Cut out the hard core and then slice the pineapple into half-moon shapes.

Cut the mangoes into long strips, about 2 cm / ¾ inch wide. Slice the oranges into rounds or separate them into segments, holding them over a bowl as you do so to catch the juice. Squeeze the juice from the pith before it is discarded.

Cut the melon into quarters and get rid of as many of the seeds as you can – if it is a Charentais melon they can all be scooped out with a small spoon. Then peel each quarter and cut it into 2 or 3 pieces.

Arrange the fruit in a round glass bowl. Sprinkle the juice of half a lemon or lime over all. Cover the bowl with cling-film and keep it in a cool place.

Halve 4 of the passion fruit and scoop the flesh, including the seeds, into a sieve over a small bowl. With a spoon, press the juice through the sieve and discard the dry seeds. Mix the passion fruit juice with that of the oranges saved earlier, plus all the juice of the one remaining orange. Finally, add to the bowl the juice and seeds of the two remaining passion fruit. Stir the juices with a fork so that the passion fruit seeds are more or less evenly distributed, and pour the contents of the bowl over all the fruit.

Serve straight away or, if you are not ready to serve, keep the bowl of fruit on top of a larger bowl filled with ice cubes.

sweet rice and mango
People in rice-growing countries do not think it strange to eat rice as a main course and rice again for dessert. In fact, in Southeast Asia we serve this not just as a dessert but as a sweet snack at any time. Why not try it instead of your usual lunch? To make sure your rice has the right consistency, use the same cup to measure the rice and the coconut milk.

for 6-8

2½ cups of coconut milk
a pinch of salt
2 tbsp caster sugar
2 cups of white glutinous rice, soaked in cold water for 1 hour, then drained
4 small or 2 large ripe mangoes

Put the coconut milk, salt and sugar in a saucepan. Bring to the boil and, when boiling, add the drained rice. Stir once and simmer, uncovered, until all the liquid has been absorbed by the rice. Remove from heat, and cover the pan. Leave it to stand for 5 minutes.

Transfer the rice to a steamer or double saucepan, and steam for 15–20 minutes.

Peel the mangoes and cut the flesh into slices or cubes.

To serve: one method is to put the rice into individual moulds or ramekins. It is advisable to line the ramekins with cling-film so that the rice can be unmoulded easily, then serve with the fruit around the little mounds. Alternatively, put a portion of unmoulded rice in the middle of each dessert plate and arrange the slices or cubes of mango around it. You could even press or roll the rice evenly on a tray lined with cling-film, then cut the rice into diamond-shaped pieces. Arrange the diamonds on the serving plate, with the mango pieces on top and around them.

steamed coconut cup cake
In Indonesia this is called 'putu ayu' or 'pretty cup cake'. Little cakes like these are popular all over Southeast Asia, not as a dessert but as a snack eaten any time between meals. In particular, they are served with tea whenever friends or neighbours call. No one ever makes an appointment to do this, so every household should have a little stock of cakes ready to offer anyone who drops in for a chat.

Traditionally, these cakes are fairly solid in Indonesia, but I like to make them lighter, principally by beating the eggs. If using fresh coconut, one will be sufficient to make the coconut milk (see page 179) and to supply the grated coconut flesh. As a mould, I use Chinese tea cups without handles, but small ramekins or ring moulds, or any small cup-shaped moulds made of aluminium, will do just as well.

makes 10-12 small cakes

5 eggs
4 tbsp caster sugar
85 g / 3 oz rice flour
30 g / 1 oz plain flour
150 ml / ¼ pint thick coconut milk
pinch of salt
115 g / 4 oz grated coconut flesh

Beat the eggs and the sugar until they are thick and pale in colour. Sift in the flours and continue beating while you slowly add the coconut milk and salt. Continue beating this batter for about 3 minutes longer.

Heat some water in a steamer and, when boiling, put 10–12 cups into the steamer basket to warm for about 2 minutes.

Divide the grated coconut evenly among the cups, pressing it in with a spoon. Then pour in equal portions of the batter. Steam for 10 minutes.

Turn out the cakes as soon as the cups are cool enough to handle.

young coconut cake

Ten years or so ago, when I was researching in the Philippines for my Rice Book, *I came across an abundance of pies in and around Manila in which the filling was the flesh of young coconuts. I believe these are still very popular. The local name for them is 'buko pie', and there are buko pie stalls everywhere, with many variations on the basic recipe. For example, the pie can become a cake simply by omitting the short-crust pastry casing. It is that variation that I describe here.*

The main ingredient is the thin layer of soft flesh that is easily scraped out of a very young coconut after the water has been poured off and drunk. Some Thai shops in Western cities sell these young nuts. Their shells, at the top, are easy enough to chop open, so that you can put a straw in and suck out the sweet liquid, but cutting the thick fibrous shell in half is not so simple. The solution is to buy young coconut flesh, in packets, from the freezer of an Oriental supermarket.

The spiny plants **pandan**, *pandanus or screwpine (Pandanus odorus) produce long, tender, aromatic leaves, delicately perfumed with a scent that has been compared to that of newly cut hay or new rice. In the West, pandanus leaves can be found in Asian food shops, sometimes cut into short strips and sealed in plastic packets, sometimes left whole and bundled together in threes or fours. For most home-cooked dishes, one piece of leaf about 5 cm / 2 inches long is sufficient. Therefore, buy as little as you can and freeze the surplus.*

for 6–8

4 large eggs
150 g / 5 oz caster sugar
115–175 g / 4–6 oz frozen young coconut strands, thawed completely before use
115 ml / 4 fl oz thick coconut milk
a large pinch of salt
115 g / 4 oz plain flour
2 tbsp melted butter, plus more for the cake tin
1 pandanus leaf, cut across into 3

Preheat the oven to 180°C / 350°F / Gas 4 and generously butter the sides and bottom of a 20-cm / 8-inch diameter cake tin, preferably one with a removable bottom.

Whisk the eggs and sugar until fluffy and light in colour. Add to this the young coconut, the coconut milk and the salt, and mix well. Sift in the flour, again mixing it well with a metal spoon. Finally, stir in the melted butter.

Lay the strips of pandanus leaf on the bottom of the prepared cake tin. Pour the cake mixture into the tin and bake it in the preheated oven for about 35–40 minutes, or until the cake is well set and slightly brown on top.

Leave it to cool for a little before lifting it out of the tin.

Indonesian spiced layered cake

This Dutch recipe has been popular in Indonesia for so long that we now regard it as our own, and serve it as a treat for Lebaran (the end of Ramadan) as well as at Christmas. Its Indonesian name lapis legit *roughly translates as 'scrummy layered cake'. The Dutch name,* spekkoek, *is also still used in Indonesia. It is a very rich cake and should be served in small, thin slices, which are easier to cut if you make your* spekkoek *in a square tin. These slices are delicious when served as petits fours with an after-dinner cup of strong coffee.*

**Makes one 20-23 cm
(8-9 inch) cake**

450 g / 1 lb unsalted butter
a drop of vanilla extract
225 g / 8 oz caster sugar
18 medium or size 2 eggs, separated
3 tbsp top of the milk
150 g / 5 oz plain flour
a pinch of salt
2 tsp freshly grated nutmeg
4 tsp ground cinnamon
1 tsp ground cloves
1 tsp ground mace
a pinch of ground white pepper (optional)

Beat the butter, vanilla and half the sugar until creamy. In another bowl, beat the egg yolks with the remaining sugar until creamy and thick. Beat these mixes together and add the milk. Sift the flour into the bowl, and fold it in carefully. Beat the whites of 8 of the eggs (use the rest for soufflés or meringues) with the salt until stiff and fold in. Stir in all the spices and mix well, but gently.

Heat a grill to its maximum temperature and preheat the oven to 150°C/300°F/Gas 2 (if using a grill inside an oven, preheat the oven and turn it off before turning on the grill). Butter a 20–23 cm (8–9 inch) square cake tin, preferably with a loose bottom.

Pour a layer of the batter about 3 mm / ⅛ inch thick over the bottom of the tin. Grill for 2 minutes until the batter has set firm. Take it from under the grill, brush the surface of the cake with melted butter, and press it flat with the bottom of a tumbler. Pour the same amount of batter again into the tin, grill and continue the same process until all the batter is used up. A good lapis legit will consist of 12–14 layers, or more. The heat of the grill browns the top of each layer, giving the cut cake its neat horizontal stripes.

Finish cooking the cake in the preheated oven for 10 minutes.

Remove the cake from the tin and allow to cool on a wire rack. It will keep moist and fresh in a cake tin or in the fridge for a week, well wrapped in greaseproof paper and an outer layer of foil. It can also be frozen.

coconut cream rice and almonds *This is one of many Oriental dishes made with rice flour. It is delicious with a summer fruit salad or with my own favourite combination of mangoes in passion fruit juice. The rice should really be freshly ground. If you have a food processor, this is no problem at all.*

for 8-10

115 g / 4 oz Thai fragrant or basmati rice, rinsed then soaked in 225 ml / 8 fl oz water for at least 8 hours or overnight
1 litre / 1¾ pints very thick coconut milk
175 g / 6 oz granulated sugar
115 g / 4 oz ground almonds

for the mango and passion fruit (optional)
2–3 ripe mangoes, peeled and the flesh cubed
juice of 1 lime
2 tsp sugar
10–12 passion fruit
2 tbsp dark rum (optional)

In a food processor, blend the rice with the water in which it has been soaked to a smooth, runny paste. Heat the coconut milk in a non-stick pan. When it is on the point of boiling, pour in the rice paste and stir almost continuously for 15 minutes while it simmers. Add the sugar and stir for 10 minutes more. Finally add the ground almonds and stir continuously for 10 more minutes.

Divide the mixture among 8–10 dessert bowls, big enough to be only half-filled by the creamy sauce. Chill for at least 4 hours before serving.

If making the mango topping, put the mango cubes in a glass bowl and mix in the lime juice and sugar. Halve the passion fruits and squeeze the juice and seeds into another bowl, reserving the juice and seeds of 1 passion fruit. Sieve the bulk of the juice and seeds into the bowl of mangoes. Mix the reserved juice and seeds into the strained juice. Add the rum, if using, and perhaps a little more sugar to taste. This can also be prepared in advance and chilled, but it should be served at room temperature. Top the bowls of rice with the fruit mix to serve.

What to drink

Conventionally, in an Asian restaurant you order beer, but this habit is being challenged, and with good reason. Chilled lager is not a logical choice to accompany food that usually has a starchy base (rice), well-marked savoury flavours, and a carefully-balanced mix of spices. The sweetness of the beer kills the spicing, its glacial coldness numbs the palate and throat without effectively absorbing the heat of the chillies, and when the carbon dioxide gas hits your stomach and wants to get out it will make you feel bloated and uncomfortable.

In fine-dining restaurants it is not uncommon to be offered a tasting menu of seven or eight courses, each with a carefully selected wine to accompany it. I don't know if it's coincidence or not, but New World wines seem to match Asian flavours remarkably well, and I have eaten some superb meals of this type in Jakarta, Sydney, Vancouver, Bangkok and Singapore. It's true that for the tourist in most Asian countries wine is very expensive, but a few enterprising people in Thailand are now growing well-recognized grape varieties and producing very fair table wines.

For everyday drinking with Asian food, I usually go either for a sharp-tasting white wine, such as a Riesling or a Sauvignon Blanc, or a fruity full-bodied red. A sparkling wine is always successful – champagne, or (at a more reasonable price) one of the dry, crisp-tasting wines that are made in the Veneto region of Italy from the Prosecco grape.

Now, chillies: in this book, I have deliberately kept the chilli count low, but however chilli-hot you like your food you will find that the capsaicin in the chilli merely inflames the tender skin lining your mouth and throat. It does not affect your taste buds, and you can therefore continue to taste the wine. (Different varieties of chilli also have different flavours, of course, so chilli and wine can affect each other that way.)

Acknowledgements

I am grateful to many people and organizations who have helped me write this book. Alas, I only have space to mention a few by name.

To start with, some hotels: the *Four Seasons/Regent Hotels* – in Singapore, Thailand, Jakarta and Bali; *Hilton International* in Adelaide; *Sutton Place* in Vancouver; the *Raffles* in Singapore and its sisters, *Le Royal* in Phnom Penh and the *Grand Hotel d'Angkor* in Siem Reap; the *Strand* in Yangon; the *Oriental* in Bangkok; the *Mandarin Oriental* in Hong Kong; the *Dorchester* in London. General managers, food and beverage managers, executive chefs and sous-chefs, PR managers, concierges – everyone in these establishments went out of their way to answer questions, find contacts and make sure that my most unreasonable wishes came true.

Likewise with restaurants: as well as the three chefs and chef-proprietors to whom this book is dedicated, I must mention John Dunham and Beh Kim Un, with their incomparable trio of restaurants in Melbourne; in the same city, Duré Dara and Stephanie Alexander; in Adelaide, Genevieve Harris of *Nediz*; in Sydney, Serge Dansereau, of the *Bathers Pavilion*, Neil Perry of *Rockpool*, and David Thompson of *Sailors Thai* (now also of *Nahm* in London). In New Zealand, Michael Lee-Richards in Christchurch. On the US and Canadian West Coast, Charles Phan of the *Slanted Door* in San Francisco, Su-mei Yu of *Saffron* in San Diego, Mai Pham of *Lemongrass* in Sacramento, Philip Chu of *Nan Yang Restaurant* in Oakland, and Sinclair and Frédérique Philip at my very favourite small hotel and restaurant, *Sooke Harbour House* on Vancouver Island. On the US East Coast, Romy Dorotan and Amy Besa of *Cendrillon* in New York, and Longteine de Monteiro and her family who own and run the *Elephant Walk* restaurants in Boston. In the UK, I must mention Peter Gordon, of the *Providores Restaurant and Tapa Room* in London. And I must not forget my long-time friend, the amazingly creative entrepreneur William W. Wongso in Jakarta, and my Balinese friends, both equally remarkable in their own ways, Anak Agung Gede Rai and Ni Wayan Murni.

Then there are my fellow-writers and teachers. I think especially of the late Barbara Tropp in San Francisco, home also of Niloufer King and Tricia Robinson. Elsewhere in North America, Madhur Jaffrey, Mary Jane Gagan, Nathan Fong, Naomi Duguid and her husband Jeffrey Alford, Lan Anh Phung, and Barbara Wheaton and colleagues at the Schlesinger Library. In Malaysia, Celine Marbeck of *Melaka*. In the Philippines, Doreen Fernandez, a great writer on food and many other subjects. In Australia, Joyce Westrip in Perth; Diana Marsland, Maureen McKeon and Diane Holuigue in Melbourne; Cherry Ripe and Gae Pincus in Sydney, and Barbara Santich in Adelaide. In New Zealand, Lauraine Jacobs, Catherine Bell, and Pip Duncan. In France, Liz Nicol and Sue Young. In the UK, Philip Iddison, who has done pioneer research into Thai foods, Alan Davidson, Richard Hosking and Roz Denny – the list could go on and on.

I must include my publisher, Quadrille, including my editor, Lewis Esson, creative director Mary Evans, designer Jim Smith, editorial assistant Katie Ginn, and Jane Suthering, who cooked my recipes most beautifully for Georgia Glynn Smith to photograph. Finally, I must not forget to include big thank-yous to Anne Furniss, the commissioning editor, to my agent, John McLaughlin, and as always to my husband Roger – and to many more friends, whose help and kindness I cannot mention here but will never forget.

Bibliography

I have found the following reference works especially useful:

Isaac Burkill, *Dictionary of Economic Products of the Malay Peninsula*
(1935, republished by the Ministry of Agriculture and Co-operatives on behalf
of the governments of Malaysia and Singapore, Kuala Lumpur, 1966)

Alan Davidson, *The Oxford Companion to Food* (OUP, London and New York, 1999)

Joy Larkcom, *Oriental Vegetables* (London, John Murray, 1991)

Jill Norman, *The Complete Book of Spices* (Dorling Kindersley, London, 1990)

Anne Willan, *Reader's Digest Complete Guide to Cookery* (Dorling Kindersley, London, 1989)

Recommended for further reading:

Jeffrey Alford and Naomi Duguid, *Hot Sour Salty Sweet* (Artisan, New York, 2000).
Based on the authors' extensive travels in the valley of the Mekong.

Michael Bailes, *The Fragrant Chilli* (Kangaroo Press, East Roseville, NSW, 1999)

David Burton, *Savouring the East* (Faber, London, 1996)

Andrew Dalby, *Dangerous Tastes* (British Museum Press, London, 2000).
The history of the spice business from about 500 BC almost to the present day.

Serge Dansereau, *Food & Friends* (HarperCollins, Sydney, 1998).
A great Australian chef writes about food and wine in Europe.

Sasha Judelson, ed., *East West Food* (Hamlyn, London, and SOMA Books, San Francisco, 1997)

Cheong Liew, with Elizabeth Ho, *My Food* (Allen & Unwin, St Leonards, NSW, 1995)

Longteine de Monteiro and Katherine Neustadt, *The Elephant Walk Cookbook*
(Houghton Mifflin, Boston and New York, 1998).
Cambodian dishes from the menus of the Elephant Walk restaurants in Boston.

Sri Owen, *The Rice Book* (Frances Lincoln, London, 1998)

Sri Owen, *Indonesian Regional Food and Cookery* (Frances Lincoln, London, 1999)

Sri Owen, *Noodles: the New Way* (Quadrille, London, 2000)

Neil Perry, *Rockpool* (Heinemann Australia, Melbourne, 1996).
Dishes from a great and innovative Sydney restaurant.

Mai Pham, *Pleasures of the Vietnamese Table* (HarperCollins, New York, 2001)

Joanna Simon, *Wine with Food* (Mitchell Beazley, London, 1996)

Nusara Thaitawat, *The Cuisine of Cambodia* (Nusara & Friends, Bangkok, 2000)

Tetsuya Wakuda, *Tetsuya* (HarperCollins, Sydney, 2001).
As in Tetsuya's restaurant, every dish is accompanied by a wine recommendation.

Alice Waters, *Chez Panisse Vegetables* (HarperCollins, New York, 1996)
and *Chez Panisse Café Cookbook* (HarperCollins, New York, 1999)

Martin Yan, *Martin Yan's Asia* (KQED, San Francisco, 1997)

Su-Mei Yu, *Cracking the Coconut* (HarperCollins, New York, 2000)

Index

Page numbers in *italic* refer
to the illustrations